I0468234

The $ix-Figure Writer

Copyright © 2016 by Michael Ashley and Sham Shivaie

All rights reserved. No part of this book may be used or reproduced in any manner whatsoever without written permission except in the case of brief quotations embodied in critical articles and reviews.

ISBN-10: 1523992786

ISBN-13: 978-1523992782

ASIN: B01BN0N05C

Edited by: Lorna Collins

Cover Design by: Sommer Stewart

The $ix-Figure Writer

by

Michael Ashley

and

Sham Shivaie

TABLE OF CONTENTS

INTRODUCTION

This book's purpose can be summed up in one word: empowerment. It is a unique self-help book for writers authored by two six-figure earning writers.

Michael offers experience from the content creation side.

Sham brings marketing knowledge to sell your writing services. At times our expertise overlaps, offering you the best of both worlds to help you to monetize your craft.

At the beginning of each chapter, we will identify the author.

Our Value Proposition

Successful entrepreneurs don`t start businesses. They solve problems. They don`t create companies. They create solutions. If you look at the most successful tech start-ups, you'll see they were formed to solve a problem. Uber provides a better solution for transportation. Airbnb provides a better solution for traveling. GoPro provides a better solution for capture exciting moments.

The goal of this book is very much the same: to provide a solution to the problem facing many aspiring and experienced writers: How can I make money doing this?

We set out to create an instructional book that any writer could use to achieve an annual six-figure income.

Our guiding principle for this material was centered on two questions:

- What would we want to read to achieve our goals?
- What would we want to know?

In summary, we wrote this book because when we were first starting out, we would have loved to have had a blueprint like this to learn from.

Michael's Story

I am an academically trained writer who has worked professionally.

While studying at the University of Missouri, I got my first professional writing assignment as a reporter for the *Columbia Missourian* during my senior year. My undergraduate major was Philosophy. I minored in Journalism. Usually, the prestigious "J" School won't let you be a reporter unless you're a Journalism major, but I earned an exception through hard work and knowing somebody. (By the way, both are helpful items for any aspiring *$ix-Figure Writer*.)

The year before, I had studied abroad in London. When I returned to the States, I dated an editor who worked for the paper. She thought I possessed writing talent so she convinced the editors to let me fill in over Christmas break while the usual staff members were on vacation. (Again, this experience indicates what it takes to break in as a writer. Often, you must work free with no idea if it's going to pay off.)

I ended up writing the articles that no one else wanted, like obituaries. My work impressed the editors enough that they bent the rules and took me on as a full-fledged reporter. Though they gave me a local beat for a small town no one else wanted, I turned what could have been a boring assignment into compelling, dramatic articles. Some even made the front page (above the flap). Upon graduating, I evaluated my career prospects as a journalist. They weren't good. The best annual salary I could expect was $30,000. I didn't want to be poor, so I took a job as a mortgage broker.

Even though I was making all my monthly sales goals, I felt unsatisfied. I knew my passion was writing. More than anything, I wanted to be a screenwriter. After three years in the workforce, I applied to Chapman University's Master of Fine Arts Screenwriting program, was accepted, and moved across the country.

Since I had experience working in the corporate sector between my undergraduate and graduate years, I knew how precious an educational hiatus would be. I took full advantage of the opportunity and threw myself into every aspect of my MFA writing education. I wrote screenplays for class, which weren't expected of me. (A famous actor optioned one of them.) I interned as a script reader for a production company. Throughout it all, I networked like crazy, meeting people who would eventually help in my career as a professional screenwriter when I finished school.

Unfortunately, I graduated in 2007, just as the writers' strike plagued Hollywood. It sucked. No studio was hiring new writers, especially recent graduates. The only entertainment jobs I could find were assistant positions at movie studios, rolling calls for abusive executives.

However, because I had interned for Cindy Cowan Entertainment as a reader while at Chapman, I had professional experience reading scripts and writing coverage. (Coverage is a term the entertainment industry uses. Overworked agents and executives pay readers to read material to tell them if it's good or not.)

I became a reader for Creative Artists Agency, where I worked under Cathy Tarr, the head of the Literary Department. I was paid $50 per script and a little more per book to give my thoughts on volumes of material. (No kidding. I read over 500 screenplays in my two years at CAA.) I consider my time there as a kind of second grad school. I learned on the job how to determine what makes a successful narrative. Richard Lovett, CAA's president, liked my coverage and frequently requested me to read for him.

Reading scripts for famous actors may sound glamorous, but it pays lousy, so I had to take another job. Trading on my experiences in finance, I landed a position as a commercial insurance broker. This may sound insane to someone who doesn't understand the drive of an aspiring writer, but at one point in my twenties, I 1) worked forty hours a week as an insurance broker, 2) read five-to-ten screenplays per week as a reader, 3) wrote my own feature/TV screenplays, and 4) produced/screen wrote a web series I also acted in. In addition, I had a girlfriend and a social life. Looking back, I don't know how I did it.

My first break came in 2011 when I was selected to be part of Disney's Brainstorm Group. Six young screenwriters were picked to work with Gary Marsh, Disney's president, for one week to generate story ideas they could use to make their next movie. The treatment I wrote with another screenwriter named Michelle was the only one picked. It was later turned into the 2012 Halloween movie, *Girl Versus Monster.*

This consulting assignment was the first time I earned big bucks as a screenwriter. It gave me the confidence to leave my corporate job and strike out on my own as a fulltime writer. I began acquiring diverse gigs: screenwriting assignments, screenplay consultations, journalistic articles, blogs, ghostwriting commissions and copywriting work. The key to it all was leveraging my past successes to get the next job. When someone who didn't know me (and consequently didn't value me as a writer) asked if I was qualified, I simply stated my past credits. Then I worked as hard as I could to prove my worth.

In 2014, I was commissioned to write a children's novel in the vein of *Percy Jackson.* How it all happened was very romantic. I was flown to Marin County for a job interview to screen write and produce an animated series. It centered on explaining difficult scientific concepts concerning evolution to young people. I got the job, but the project morphed into every aspiring novelist's dream. I was paid to co-write the first book in a children's fantasy book series.

For the next year, I wrote my heart out eight-to-ten hours a day, Monday through –Friday, and even on weekends. I completed the manuscript after many revisions in the spring of 2015. My co-author and I queried agents and editors to publish the material and were lucky enough to get a top agent and editor to request the manuscript. As I write this, it's currently being read with an eye toward publication in the next year.

So why did I just tell you this detailed story? To demonstrate three things:

- Writing is a hard industry to break into.
- Every writer's journey is complicated and specific.
- It's possible to achieve success as a writer if you possess ambition, a strong work ethic, and creativity.

By sharing my own journey, experiences, and advice, I hope you will see it is truly possible to make a successful and fulfilling living as a *$ix-Figure Writer*. Good luck, and I hope this book changes your life.

Sham's Story

I often like to joke I'm an entrepreneur by trade and a starving writer at heart.

Believe it or not, there are many similarities between entrepreneurship and writing. For starters, neither of them offers much rest. The brain of a writer and the entrepreneur must be laser-focused. Each enterprise requires creativity, outside-the-box thinking, and unrelenting drive.

For a long time, I identified myself as an entrepreneur and marketer. Yet, my writing itch continued to grow. So, like any good entrepreneur, I found a way to capitalize on my passion: launching my own blog in the spring of 2015. The blog focused on the electronic cigarette/vapor industry, the industry I'd built my company in. After opening multiple specialty "vape shops" and launching my own branded line of products, I began blogging to cover news and current events about that sector. Within six months, it grew from a humble means of expression to a thriving digital media platform with thousands of followers, a global readership and a monthly reach in the millions.

At that point, I realized I could write *and* build a business.

How did I do it? You'll soon find out the details, but it all came down to marketing. I'm not the best writer, but I am a good marketer, and I know how to brand.

I started my first business when I was seventeen, organizing and promoting a local teen nightclub. I rented out a local rec center, hired a DJ, and passed out flyers. It quickly became a hit, earning me a lot of money. It's quite a feeling to be seventeen years old and pulling in three thousand dollars in a night.

The business led me to work in the nightlife industry. I wasn't old enough to go to nightclubs (though fake IDs and a good editing suite fixed that), yet here I was organizing events and concerts with a thousand plus in attendance. I understood little about business or marketing back then. Still, the benefit of youth is what you lack in experience you make up for in grit.

On the other hand, the downside is feeling invincible and getting cocky. When I was twenty-one, I took all my savings and invested in my first brick and mortar business. I thought I was a brilliant businessman. Having studied martial arts since I was little, I bought a struggling studio, thinking I could turn it around. I took out loans, got my parents to lend me money, and did an expensive remodel. I added all kinds of classes, from Yoga to MMA, and fantasized about how soon I'd make half a million a year. Within months, the business failed and I found myself at twenty-one near bankrupt.

Why did it fail? Because I did nothing to market it. I disregarded all my previous marketing experience. Stupidly, I thought since we had an "open" sign, customers would magically appear. There's an important lesson here for making a living as a writer. Many writers assume just because they *can* write, they'll magically succeed.

The failure of my business had a profound impact on me. After shutting things down, I committed myself to learning marketing. I read countless books, took seminars, and absorbed everything I could about advertising, branding, SEO, and copywriting.

I bounced back from the martial arts studio debacle and soon found myself consulting for other businesses. The timing was right. This was during the initial rise of social media. I built a successful consulting business helping businesses and entrepreneurs with their marketing and branding. In retrospect, I realize just how much actual writing was involved. But at the time, I never considered writing ad copy to actually count as *writing*. I pictured a writer as someone who sits at a café writing a novel, hoping to take it to a publisher.

After consulting for a number of years, I jumped back into entrepreneurship by starting a few different businesses and selling them. Eventually those enterprises brought me to my current industry: the controversial, but booming e-cigarette business.

I launched my digital publication with the intent of building a large audience, not just writing articles. I devoted time every day to writing, but I devoted more time to marketing and branding. Please understand, I didn't build a global reader base due to my awesome writing skills. I achieved success by making it my goal to get eyeballs, not accolades.

I have a genuine passion for content creation, strategy and branding. But what really drives me is combining writing, entrepreneurship, and marketing. I love the creative and logistical challenges. Understanding how to brand and create value through content has been the cornerstone of my business strategy. Now I want to share my knowledge with you.

WHY WE WROTE THIS BOOK

But First, The Backstory

Sham

Michael and I met through Jeff, my childhood best friend who is a very talented and successful entrepreneur in his own right. Jeff started holding regular Mastermind meetings at his place on Friday nights. First coined by marketer Napoleon Hill, the idea behind the Mastermind group is simple: Two heads are better than one. By aligning yourself with likeminded people, you can collectively tackle problems with exponentially more effectiveness.

Nestled away at his place high in the hills of Corte Madera, Marin County, under the shadow of Mount Tamalpais, Jeff gathered hand-picked individuals to discuss and trade ideas and offer advice. One day, I remember Jeff telling me how he planned to have a writer come the following week. I was excited because my online publication was growing, and I wanted to improve my writing abilities. I was a skilled blogger, but I wanted to be a skilled writer.

Michael and I hit it off immediately, and I was eager to share my ideas with him and get his feedback. I'm a firm believer in surrounding myself with people better than I am at things I want to improve in.

If you want to get better at business, socialize with successful business people. If you want to get fit, spend time with fit and active people.

I was eager to network with Michael and learn from him. We had instant rapport over our shared love of writing and storytelling. I was fascinated by his experiences and knowledge as a professional writer. He was intrigued by my insight and ideas on marketing and branding.

Superheroes Team Up

During one of our Mastermind meetings, Jeff needed help creating the marketing strategy for the new company he was launching. Specifically, he needed a script written for the animated video to be shown on his homepage to convey his brand. He didn't just want it to be instructional. He envisioned something engaging and entertaining.

Michael and I got to it. Together, we came up with not only an entire content strategy, but we also banged out a video script in a few hours. He had the skill and expertise to tell a cohesive and engaging story. I had the knowledge of how to use words to grab attention and sell, while also spotlighting the product's benefits.

We were able to combine our "super powers" to create an engaging narrative, which not only entertained, but could be used to convert.

This was the first time I had collaborated with an actual writer. As a consultant, I had done plenty of work with marketing teams, but they always looked at creativity as a numbers game. They were worried about "deliverables". With Michael, co-creating was this fun experience. It combined my love for storytelling with my interest in branding and strategy.

Afterward, Michael and I began brainstorming other ways to collaborate. Since so many of our conversations centered on the business of successful writing, content creation, and growing an audience, we thought: Why not write a book combining our knowledge?

We had both been fortunate to achieve six-figure incomes a year from writing, but from different approaches. We felt we could bring value to others by sharing our combined knowledge, ideas, and stories. We recognize there isn't just one specific way to become a *$ix-Figure Writer*.

We Are Here to Shift Your Paradigm

People think starting a business is hard. They think entrepreneurs are brave to take such risks. They're right. But if you ask me, being a writer is harder. It takes true bravery. Entrepreneurs can shield themselves with their businesses. They have a protective layer. Writers on the other hand, must be willing to bare their souls and allow total vulnerability.

Nevertheless, writers could take a big lesson from entrepreneurs. The biggest paradigm-shift principle is this: *mere writing is not enough.* Actual success comes from discovering how to build an audience for your writing. It's the key distinction between success and failure.

Think about it this way. You could write the most brilliant, page-turning novel ever, but if nobody reads it, what good does it do? Similarly, you could launch an incredible blog and post a new article every day filled with the most inspiring words ever written. But if no one knows it exists, if you haven't built an audience to actually read it, then what's the point? (Unless, you just like reading your own words.)

The point is this: the ability to write words is important. But the ability to *sell* those words is *more important*. And more difficult. The most successful bloggers aren't writers, they're marketers.

I built my digital publication not because of the quality of my writing, but my ability to build an audience for it.

This is Your Wake-Up Call

In order to become a *$ix-Figure Writer,* you must shift your perspective to embrace the above paradigm. Too many writers want to make a living writing but don't want to treat their writing as a business. Stop thinking it isn't necessary.

This book isn't about your hobby. It's your key to break free of the rat race. Do you crave work to deliver satisfaction, not boredom and indifference? Do you want to spend your time doing something you actually enjoy *and* earn enough income to give you the freedom to make your own schedule?

What makes you a writer? Your own beliefs do.

You have to own your identity. What makes you a writer is not necessarily a book deal with a major publisher. Nor is it making millions a year from getting your script green-lit for production. Those successes might make you feel like a "successful" writer. But the title is there for the picking for *anyone* who has the love of the craft along with the commitment to make their living from it.

Have the guts and confidence to proclaim to yourself: "I am a writer." Despite what society says, what your family tells you, or anyone else who tries to limit you with their beliefs, you are a writer the moment you decide to share your ideas with the world.

A Blueprint for Success

The following is a result of our own experiences working together and learning from each other. Michael and I have created a blueprint for anyone with a similar desire to build a successful and profitable career as a wordsmith. Ours is both a system and philosophy, which views writing as a business with an emphasis on marketing and branding.

Plenty of books on writing and books on marketing can be found for sale. Our objective is to distill the best of both worlds into a simple guide any aspiring writer can follow and practice.

In a sense, we wrote this book for ourselves because it offers answers to problems we've both experienced. Michael is a trained writer, who wanted to learn to market and sell his services. Sham is an entrepreneur and marketer, who wanted to improve his ability to write and share his ideas. Our approach combines our separate expertise.

This book explains not just how to be a writer, but how to make money writing. You need to do both in order to succeed. Being a talented writer is not enough. You need to build an audience. Likewise, being able to market and build an audience requires providing engaging and valuable content.

The *$ix-Figure Writer* Approach Will Maximize Your Success

Plenty of marketers offer their poorly written $1.99 ebooks on Amazon. They may know how to build a social media following, but who's going to read the content if it's terrible? It's not the path to building an audience. It's the way to create a bunch of disgruntled customers.

Allow me to be blunt. I am a marketer. Therefore, I feel comfortable criticizing my tribe. Far too many marketers have terrible writing abilities. They peddle poorly written self-published ebooks. The marketing world is saturated with individuals who think because they know how to build lead generation funnels or promote themselves on Facebook they qualify as writers. And you should read their work.

At the same time, plenty of copywriters think because they have read David Ogilvy's books cover-to-cover they're qualified to be writers. And plenty of passionate but delusional writers think their work will lead to financial prosperity just because they can write. Many a struggling novelist or blogger has given up prematurely because they couldn't find a publisher willing to publish their work.

This book dispenses with antiquated notions and tired, worn-out thinking.

The *$ix-Figure Writer* mentality is different. Unlike writers from the past, today's writers are trying to make their living through their writing. These individuals know how to build an actual business from writing and do so. The *$ix-Figure Writer* is different. We are hybrid creatures, combining our passion and commitment to the writing craft with the strategic and tactical thinking of an entrepreneur. The *$ix-Figure Writer* knocks out 10,000 words a day consistently while self-branding on social media.

Our goal is straightforward. We want to empower you to make money by writing words, to help you create a secure and prosperous lifestyle by doing something you truly love and are passionate about.

HOW TO USE THIS BOOK

Mental Masturbation is Fun but Unproductive

Michael

When I talk to buddies I went to college with, one of their chief complaints is about how all the money they spent did little to prepare them professionally. The biggest problem with getting a degree is the educational paradigm is centered on *theory*. When it comes to the practicalities of making a living, educational programs fail to prepare the student.

Let me assure you this book will not do that.

The purpose of this book is to provide practical tools to help you succeed as a *$ix-Figure Writer*. Life is hard enough. The last thing Sham or I want is to waste your time. Promising to help you and then delivering nothing but trite platitudes, such as: "Work hard", "Avoid distractions" and "Write every day," would be a betrayal.

You already know you need to do those things if you are a professional writer. You don't need us to tell you. Every self-help book on writing emphasizes the importance of consistent writing. It doesn't bear repeating.

What you need is a guide about *how to succeed as a writer*. This book offers you practical suggestions on how to monetize your writing. I offer the following suggestions on how to use it.

Read the Book Through the First Time for Pleasure

I'm not joking. Read this book the whole way through one time to enjoy it. This is for a practical reason. Adults teach important lessons to children through engaging parables. People, especially little kids, gravitate toward conflict-laden narratives starring interesting characters. Any parent who has read a story to their child knows this. If you offer them a good tale, no kid can resist wanting to know what happens next.

As Dave Kost, my excellent screenwriting professor, once told our class, "The brains of human beings are hard-wired for stories." Our minds best understand life through storytelling. We absorb and recall things better if we think of them in narrative terms with a beginning, middle, and an end. Therefore, the reason I suggest you read this book straight through as something to be enjoyed, like a story, is you will retain the fundamentals if you relax and let the words wash over.

The Spirit of the Book, Not the Letter

Why doesn't it matter if you don't get it all the first time? What's paramount is to absorb the *spirit* of the material. If you glean the broad strokes of this book, its *essence*, it will have a transformative, positive impact on your overall thinking.

Likewise, it isn't necessary to perform each suggestion immediately to notice significant changes in your writing career. Success will come eventually if you are diligent and persistent. Look at the forest, not the trees. Liken the experience to an engaging lecture, not a homework assignment. The overall goal is paradigm shift.

Last, the two most valuable items you should now accept are:

- You are a writer the moment you say you are.
- It is possible for you to earn six figures through your writing.

The Second Time Around, Dig in Like Crazy

The next time you come back to the material, focus on the little details. All of them.

When reading the second time, imagine the material as a textbook you would use to prepare for a test. Highlight important sections. Make important notes in the margins. Quiz yourself. Write down questions to spark other ideas. Essentially, engage and fully absorb the book's contents.

To use a film metaphor, think about this book like a beloved movie you watch over and over. One such film I have seen countless times is *Goodfellas*. My brothers and I grew up hearing lines from it so often we could recite them though we had never actually watched the film. One scene in particular we knew well was the one in which Joe Pesci screams at Ray Liotta, "Am I funny? How am I funny? You mean, *I'm* a clown to amuse you?"

The first time I actually watched the movie in high school, I was blown away. I watched it for pleasure. I liked it so much I began to *study* it. I picked up little details I didn't catch the first time around, such as how Henry Hill (Liotta) is portrayed sympathetically.

It's no small feat for a screenwriter to make us like a gangster who steals and beats people for money. But they did. How? They demonstrated Henry's good heart. More than once, Henry intervenes to save someone else's life. Meanwhile, other less sympathetic characters are presented as vile because they kill for fun. Additionally, Henry acts loyally to his friends. Until the end, he never rats on them. He even goes to prison for Paulie, his father figure.

The point is the more times I watched this movie, the more aware I became of these tiny details, which made it work. I suggest you look for those when reading this book. The more times you read it, the more little details you'll pick up, broadening your overall comprehension and deepening your abilities to achieve your goal of becoming a *$ix-Figure Writer*.

It's Not Enough to Read. You Must Take Action

Does this sound familiar? You know someone who calls herself a writer. Yet when you ask her what she's working on, she offers an excuse as to why she hasn't written anything yet. This happened a lot in my MFA program, and it always baffled me. Higher education isn't cheap. It costs thousands and thousands of dollars to get a degree. Still, time and again, I witnessed fellow students blowing off their assignments. They came to class with nothing to show. It boggled my mind. They weren't taking advantage of having a captive workshop of peers to read and comment on their work. They threw their money away.

My point: don't be like ninety percent of people who call themselves writers and achieve nothing. Put into practice a discipline based on strong habits. At the end of each chapter is a summary of the major points and action steps. Follow them. They will help you get the most out of the material. In addition, complete each workbook exercise. If you do so, you will leapfrog ahead on your path to becoming a *$ix-Figure Writer.*

Also, commit to yourself to this idea: don't just follow this book's suggestions, but surpass them by creating your *own* ideas to ensure you are paid six figures for your writing.

Use Us As a Resource

We live in interesting times. Reading a book no longer has to be a one-way, passive experience. Beyond looking up items online, there are even more practical ways to turn this book into an immersive, interactive experience.

How many self-help authors do you know who actually want to hear from their readers and will work hard to see them succeed? Sham and I are committed to your success. Please feel free to write to us. If your question is something other writers may be facing, we will turn it into a blog to share with our audience.

The idea is based on the Mastermind Sessions, which brought us together. So much of writing is a solitary experience. It can often feel like you are alone with your problems. We understand and want to assist you. Just as two minds are better than one, *multiple* minds are even better. Other writers have probably dealt with or are dealing with the same issue. Sham and I will weigh in on your problem, offering you solutions from our experiences. Then we will open it up to the group to contribute their thoughts and suggestions.

Enough explanations. Let's get to the meat of this thing so you can start earning six figures from your writing.

CHAPTER 1 -
THE WRITER'S LIFE IS ALL ABOUT PERCEPTION

"There is nothing to writing. All you do is sit down at a typewriter and bleed."

~Ernest Hemingway

Here's a little game. The next time you go to a party and someone asks what you do; tell that person you are a writer. Odds are he or she will give you a funny look and ask one of two things:

1. Have you written anything I've heard of?
2. How do you make any money?

Early Influences or It'll Never Happen for You

Michael

My father's best friend in high school was Glenn Savan. When I was kid, he published his first book, *White Palace.* A bestseller set in St. Louis, Missouri, where I was raised, it eventually spawned the 1990 film starring Susan Sarandon, James Spader, and Jason Alexander.

Savan later released one more book, *Goldman's Anatomy,* before dying of a heart attack at age forty-nine. Of the two books, the latter is my favorite. Though not nearly as big a commercial success, (there were no film adaptations) it contains more character depth, romantic insight, and is all around a better story. I bring this up because it relates to perception.

Writing, unlike plumbing, is a subjective business. It's easy to tell if your toilet is broken. Recognizing a great book, on the other hand, can be nebulous. Not only is the public often divided, even so-called loyal readers will vary in their opinions. For instance, my dad thinks Savan's second book is lousy.

Writing is also dependent on the whims of time. Though *The Great Gatsby* has been canonized in our culture, recognized as the great American novel, it was not well received at first. In fact, when the book was first printed in 1925, critics hated it. Harvey Eagleton of the *Dallas Morning News* wrote, "One finishes *The Great Gatsby* with a feeling of regret, not for the fate of the people in the book but for Mr. Fitzgerald."

Apparently, readers weren't ready for it either. It sold a dismal 20,000 copies, many fewer than Fitzgerald's previous bestsellers, *This Side of Paradise* and *The Beautiful and the Damned*. Like Savan, Fitzgerald died mired in obscurity with a poorly attended funeral.

Fitzgerald is recognized as a genius today. *Gatsby* is assigned in high school English classes across the country. "Too little, too late," he'd probably say. Or, "Where were all of you back then?" The bottom line is writing is a notoriously fickle, unpredictable field. For every Tom Clancy or Stephen King, thousands, if not millions of unpublished writers exist whose works you and I have never heard of or never will.

Back to my dad and Glenn Savan. Like me, my dad is self-employed. Unlike me, he chose a "respectable profession." He's an attorney.

Remember the game I asked you to play? Think about the response you would get if you substituted the word, "lawyer" for "writer" at that party. I imagine you would get quite a different reaction if you told partygoers you were a lawyer. (Most likely, you would be met with approval, unless the person you were talking to is anything like my mom, my father's first wife, who now detests lawyers.)

I grew up hearing horror stories from my dad about how hard it was for Glenn to get his career break. While my dad was busy in his twenties buying his first house,

Glenn was busy bussing tables. My dad could afford to buy private health insurance and travel internationally in his thirties. Glenn lived with his parents until his first book sold. Even then, he didn't make enough money from the advance to qualify for a mortgage. Not until a movie studio optioned the book did Glenn see some real cash.

Based on this, you can imagine the chilly reception I got from my dad when I told him I, too, wanted to be a writer.

Don't Quit Your Day Job. It's Already Gone

Most people think earning a living from writing is somewhat equivalent to winning the lottery. It's unlikely to happen and even if it does, it probably has a lot more to do with luck than volition.

They are dead wrong on both counts.

The story about Glenn's eventual writing success occurred between the late 1980s and early 1990s. The world was a vastly different place then. The now ubiquitous Internet was conspicuously absent. But you know what *was* present? Pensions. Job security. Stable jobs offering health insurance and upward mobility based on company loyalty.

Just as Fitzgerald never saw his book's success, Glenn didn't live long enough to be vindicated for his career gamble.

In the twenty-first century, it no longer pays to play it safe by taking a so-called secure job. Even before the "jobless" recovery following the 2008 financial crash, profitable corporations stayed profitable by offshoring American jobs. The Boston-based consultancy, Forrester, estimates American jobs leave the U.S. at a rate of 12,000 to 15,000 per month. And not just industrial jobs. Once seemingly untouchable white-collar jobs in the financial sector are moving to India or being automated.

But you know what can't be automated or outsourced? The human creative mind. *The writer's mind.*

Writing: A Recession-Proof Job. *If* You Do It Right

When I tell people at parties what I do, I am inevitably barraged by the above questions. People can't believe I actually write for a living. They say things like, "But I thought writers were poor." This leads to the first *$ix-Figure Writer* Tip.

> ***$ix-Figure Writer* Tip:** To become successful, you must be *perceived* as successful.

Your Appearance Speaks Volumes Before You Do

I purposely do not dress like a shlub. If you want to make six figures as a writer, abandon the starving artist look. When I lived in LA and took development meetings, as the "talent," I was expected to dress down. "Screenwriters don't dress well," I was told. "Only agents do."

Guess what happens when you wear a t-shirt, flip-flops and jeans to a meeting. You're treated like you look. You'll be paid the amount of money a teenager earns.

A romantic notion says creatives should dress casually. Perhaps it harkens back to an ignorant belief that writers are so busy dreaming and creating we can't be bothered to properly dress ourselves.

But what you wear says a great deal. If you wear flip-flops to a business lunch at a fancy restaurant, not only do you signal your poor fashion sense, but your non-verbal body language suggests your foolishness extends to other life matters. It cries out, "Look at what a slob I am. Not only can I barely dress myself, I probably don't know how to read contracts or negotiate for myself."

Don't be daft. Dressing well will serve you well. And not just for being taken seriously as a writer. People tend to treat well-dressed individuals better than people who are not.

Just ask lawyers. They have it right. This leads me to:

> **$ix-Figure Writer Tip:** If you are not successful yet, then you *definitely* need to dress up.

Fake It 'Til You Make It

The year before I enrolled in my MFA program, I applied to be an account manager at a mortgage brokerage and somehow got the job. Until then, I had only been a loan officer. I had a loan processor to assist me with my loans, but I had never done her job (which was infinitely more technical than mine was and required experience with proprietary software I had never used.) My previous role was strictly in sales.

This new position paid much better than being a loan officer. As a loan officer, I made commission only. As an account manager, I stood to receive a hefty hourly salary, a commission, *and* a percentage of the profits from all six of my loan officers who worked under me. The problem was come Monday morning, I had to know how to process loans and pretend to have experience managing multiple brokers.

Like I said, I had somehow managed to charm my way through the interview process, but now that it was time to actually manage my new team. I knew I was woefully under qualified.

My first day was disastrous. I suspected the people working under me knew I was out of my league after I failed to answer basic questions I should have known.

Did I quit? Absolutely not. I went home and spent the night researching loan processing. I read my manual cover to cover and took copious notes. All this was helpful, but you know what helped the most?

I bought some nice suits. I also got a good-looking, expensive haircut. When I returned the next day, I changed my demeanor. Instead of looking flustered by all the new challenges, I adopted a cocky attitude, signaling I was super busy and therefore important.

I sold the persona, and it worked. Even though I didn't have the technical chops those first few weeks, I made every person believe I did by dressing and acting the part. I changed their *perception* of me. And once I did, all the other little things fell into place. The same idea applies to you as an aspiring *$ix-Figure Writer*. So what if you haven't been paid yet for a writing assignment? *Act like you have.*

People are highly impressionable creatures. What you project will become their reality. If you exhibit skittishness, nervousness or fear, they will sense it and dismiss you as an amateur. But if you come across as relaxed and competent, they will have no problem working with you. Most of all, they will have no problem *paying* you what you are worth.

EXERCISE: Change People's Perceptions About You

Here are some immediate practical activities to encourage others to view you as a *Six-Figure Writer*.

Step One: Invest in at least one new outfit to make you look good for upcoming meetings with potential clients. Buy two more as soon as you can. If you are a man, buy dress shirts and slacks (not jeans), and a pair of expensive-looking shoes. A nice blazer would be nice, too as well as a tie. If you are a woman, stock up on business suits to complement your appearance as well as nice skirts, dress slacks, dressy blouses, and dress shoes. The key for both sexes is to look professional and attractive.

Step Two: Order business cards to establish yourself as a professional writer. Don't make them cutesy. The object is to appear dignified.

Step Three: If you are in the habit of not paying attention to your personal grooming, break it. Get a stylish haircut. Men: shave or make your facial hair look neat. You are selling an image. Women: the same idea applies. Make personal grooming choices to best accentuate your appearance.

Step Four: Define your new identity on your own terms and own it. To return to the hypothetical party, if and when people ask you what you do, tell them you are a writer and make no apologies or excuses. Make a point to exude confidence and success at all times, no matter how things are going.

Final Thoughts: Writers Have the Best Job on Earth

Consider the life of author, George R.R. Martin. If you don't know who he is, put this book down, go online, and buy his *Game of Thrones* books to discover master fiction writing. Martin is responsible for creating a rich universe of characters, lands, and creatures. His books actually possess made-up religions as well as a unique and detailed cosmology. For his efforts and creativity, Martin's books have received widespread attention via HBO's adaptation into an ongoing TV series.

What does Martin get to do every day? Now I don't know the guy, but I imagine the answer is: whatever he wants. Like other fantasy heavy-hitters, such as J.K. Rowling, Martin has found a way to monetize his brand so the world is practically salivating to receive his next tasty morsel of literary goodness. Besides the exceptional financial benefits of having a winning book series, as well as a hit TV show, Martin has achieved something far greater. He is able to lead a fulfilling life on his terms.

If you remember my words from the *How To Use This Book Section* with exasperation based my assertion this book is about money, not creative shenanigans, you would be entitled to a modicum of righteous anger. This book is *not* about achieving new creative, literary heights. It is a practical guide to making a living doing what you love.

However, you must know you could be paid well through many other pursuits, most of which would be far easier than writing. But you, dear reader, chose to become a *$ix-Figure Writer*. Why? There must be many, many reasons. Undoubtedly, some of them are similar to my own. But the simplest, best reason of all, is this: *because it's fun.*

Somewhere amidst the technical aspects of monetization, networking, SEO-optimization, batching, and a whole host of other topics, this book delves into, one important consideration could get lost. *Heart.*

We writers are a rare breed. We endure all manner of setbacks, tragedies, and rejections for the sake of our ambition. This book is your practical guide to cutting your losses and leveraging your wins to grant you a successful life, but it would be woefully incomplete without a reminder of why we write.

I chose to become a writer at an early age because I loved using my imagination to create. Sometimes on long car rides, my wife, Valerie, will ask me deep questions to encourage lively conversation. Once she asked, "If you weren't a writer, what other profession would you choose?" I looked at her and said, "I wouldn't pick any other profession. Being a writer is who I am. It's all I've ever wanted to do."

So when I ask you to consider Martin's life, imagine how joyful he probably is. Of course, Martin is making far more than six figures a year. But after a certain point, the numbers don't matter. Once you are in the six-figure range, you are destined to have enough financial stability to pivot from a place of wanting to a place of being.

When I ask you to consider Martin's life, I am really asking you to envision your own potential life. What does it look like? What does it *feel* like to wake up every day with the option to do what you love?

It's fun. Right?

$ix-Figure Writer Tip: Beyond any other consideration, focus on earning the money. Being perceived well is important as a means to an end. But what truly matters are the results.

Chapter Summary

- Unlike other professions, the field of writing is highly subjective. It is largely based on the perceptions of others.
- The best way to become a successful *$ix-Figure Writer* is to transform people's perceptions of you.
- Writing, a once thankless and unpredictable vocation, has usurped seemingly safe jobs (in areas like finance, for example). The writer has an advantage over other professions because a creative mind can never be automated or outsourced.
- It is far better to adopt a "fake it 'til you make it" approach in the beginning of your *$ix-Figure Writer* career to attract positive perceptions to allow you to be successful.

Action Steps:

- Ignore antiquated appeals to "common sense" about choosing a career in writing. In the old economic paradigm, it was a risky move to select a career in writing. In the new "Connection Economy," writers have an advantage over other so-called safe professions.
- Dress for success. This includes personal grooming. Look your best to draw people to you, ensuring a professional, successful perception.
- Create business cards and begin labeling yourself as a writer.

CHAPTER 2 -
THE INTERNET CHANGED
EVERYTHING

"Without change there is no innovation, creativity, or incentive for improvement. Those who initiate change will have a better opportunity to manage the change that is inevitable."

~William Pollard

It's exciting to time to be a writing entrepreneur. Once seemingly insurmountable obstacles, such as traditional publishing, have melted away in the face of the Internet's bright and shiny new dawn. This chapter explores why your unique skillset is in constant demand and how to take advantage. It also seeks to instruct you how to define yourself to maximize your earning potential and identifies the need for audience building.

The New Reality

Sham

Before the Internet, if you wanted to make a living as a writer, you had few options to distribute your work. You either had to have a book publishing deal or submit your writing to some other existing publication, such as a magazine or newspaper.

The Internet upended the old model, putting the power to publish and distribute in your hands. The first early adaptors to this new, democratized "bottoms-up" wave were bloggers. The most successful ones utilized the web to self-publish and launch their own content platforms. Nowadays, anyone can be a one-person *Gutenberg Press* with the resources to disseminate their writing to the whole world.

Even so, just because you *can* start your own blog or self-publish your own ebook, it doesn`t mean anyone cares or is actually going to read it. It's up to *you* to earn those eyeballs. The larger point, however, is we now have the technology to distribute unlimited content through the Internet. Coupled with innovation, people now have unprecedented access to consume vast amounts of content with ease. Digital books in particular have been a revolutionary assault on traditional publishers' literary stranglehold.

So who stands to win in this new power dynamic? *$ix-Figure Writers, if* they adapt their business model to integrate the new digital reality.

News Flash: It's the Best Time Ever to Be a Writer

Pity the writers, you hear. People read fewer books than they used to. Traditional publishing is dying. Major book retail giants, such as Borders, have gone bankrupt. Remaining players, like Barnes and Noble, are struggling. In addition, people have stopped reading newspapers. They don't want them delivered to their homes, and many have already failed.

Forget the hype. Don't pity the writers. *This is the best time ever for the well-positioned.*

Yes, people read less in traditional forms. But people are consuming written digital content like crazy. And the numbers only stand to increase exponentially.

Don't' be concerned about traditional publishing's slow death. Long live content platforms. They're exploding with growth. We're living in the *Buzzfeed* era. People are reading fewer books, but they're reading more than ever. They're just reading in a new way.

$ix-Figure Writer **Tip:** Short form, blog-style articles are key writing for the new Connection Economy. Practice writing in this form to increase your attractiveness to future clients and increase business opportunities.

Content is King

Nowadays people want the following: easy to digest, value-driven content. Imbed the idea into your mind and carve it into your psyche.

What Defines Value?

Don't be depressed, but the sad truth is even trivial entertainment qualifies as value-driven content today. Like it or not, there is a kind of genius to *Buzzfeed*'s stripped down platform. It's not for nothing the company is valued in the billions. From offering listicles to sharing funny cat pictures, they're giving people what they want. *$ix-Figure Writers* don't judge what others consider quality content. They pragmatically position themselves to deliver that content.

Easy to Digest Content: 24/7 Ubiquity = 24/7 Need

People *love* to consume content. And they're consuming more than ever before. Podcast listening is exploding with subscribers. Netflix and YouTube have unleashed unfathomable numbers of videos. Amazon offers access to nearly every book ever written. What's amazing is all this content is accessible with just a few thumb motions from a device, which fits in the palm of your hand. (And, of course, an active credit card.)

For the first time in history, people now have access to an endless stream of entertainment and knowledge. And what do they want? More of it. This is why content is king.

Can you guess what *$ix-Figure Writers* are? Content Creators.

Content Creators

Writers create content. The best ones create *lots* of it, consistently. This gives us a massive edge in this new content-driven era, the Connection Economy.

You can truly become your own content producer. Think about it. As opposed to a manufacturer who has to seek out materials and/or labor, your ability to produce, *to sustain yourself*, comes entirely from your own head. It's inside of you an amazing commodity not everyone has.

The *$ix-Figure Writer* is a one-person content-generating factory.

$ix-Figure Writer Tip: Big corporations now invest more and more in content creation. As traditional advertising proves ineffective, position yourself to major brands, which have awakened to the importance of branded web content.

Are You an Artist or a Business?

It's an important existential question. If you want to make a six-figure living as a writer, you must stop thinking of yourself as an artist and start thinking of yourself a business owner. It's what you are. There are no exceptions.

If you want to write a kinky romance novel about a hot cross-dressing alien who saves the damsel in distress from a gang of ninja perverts out of pure joy for the craft of writing, go for it. If you want to author an exhaustively researched, 500-page discourse on Soren Kierkegaard's theology, by all means, do so. Heck, send me a copy, I like collecting paperweights.

But don't expect to actually earn a living from it.

I don't mean to be rude or harsh, but the brutal truth is most writers who pursue obscure literary passions need a day job. (Unless they have the luxury of holding down a tenured academic post or are independently wealthy.)

Sure, if you want to write for creative fun or intellectual pursuits, let no one stop you. You should write about what you enjoy or have an interest in. But if you want to *make money* writing, face up to the reality that you are a business.

Too many extraordinary writers get less than ordinary results because they fail to make this distinction. Or worse, they waste away in unsatisfying careers, jaded and disgruntled not to be doing what they love. Think of it this way: business before pleasure. If you actually love writing, then you must be willing to embrace this principle. Earning a living writing words should be your goal. What those words are needn't overly concern you, at least when you are starting out.

To clarify, I am not suggesting you mindlessly type away with no soul. Instead, combine both business savvy and passion for a six-figure writing income. Being a writer is not easy. Consistently delivering engaging, quality writing requires a mental endurance few have. Accomplishing this is what sets writers apart. The average person gets overwhelmed at the thought of writing a two-page essay. A writer calls it a warm-up.

But remember, you don't have to sacrifice your artistic expression in order to succeed as a writer. Just take your creative passion and integrate it into your writing business. This massive paradigm shift will cultivate the right attitude towards your chosen career path.

You Must Become a Digital Jack-of-All-Trades

Once you have accepted your identity as a business, not an artist, you must next embrace one other reality to shine in these brave new times.

A successful *$ix-Figure Writer* must be a veritable Jack-of-All-Trades. You may prefer a particular writing style, topic or genre. Some writers pen romance novels. Others author self-help books like the one you're reading. The successful *$ix-Figure Writer,* however, is the individual willing to adapt to and accommodate each opportunity.

For instance, to cash in on the demand for web-based content, it's necessary to tailor your writing not only to the format, but also to the specific tastes and views of the intended audience. Determine how to make your words consumable and engaging to the people who might read them.

In my experience, some of the best web copywriters are not advertising enthusiasts. They are, in fact, aspiring novelists struggling to pay their bills. They understand the value of their creative abilities to structure and tell engaging stories to captivate and enchant readers. As opposed to some of the more classically trained marketers who write web copy that sounds like a sales pitch, these individuals find ways to engage their readership online to build brand loyalty.

The craft of writing may be your skill, but it must be adaptable to fit the demands of your audience or clients. When selling your writing services, remember you're not writing for yourself. You're writing for others. One of the biggest hurdles most writers must overcome is coming to grips with this principle. Write for yourself in your personal diary. When writing to make an actual living, be willing to write for the audience, which is going to read it.

Strategic writing is versatile and offers multiple web-based revenue streams based on creative content. We will cover many of these later on. The important point here is to recognize the following:

- The disruptive influence of the Internet has upended the traditional publishing model.
- Those who stand to gain from the new economic reality are writers because the public demand for digital content is insatiable.
- *$ix-Figure Writers* can meet the demand by accommodating their skills to position themselves for monetary opportunity.

$ix-Figure Writer Tip: Digital writers must embrace the new reality. There are no more gatekeepers if you can leverage the power of technology to distribute your content.

Make Engagement Your Goal

I'm sure you've heard the saying, "Jack-of-all-trades, master of none."

Being a *$ix-Figure Writer* means being a Jack (or Jill) of all trades, *and a* master of one. One big, main, crucial, powerful thing: The ability to write content to engage readers. What do I mean by engagement? I mean being able to write in a way to make people actually want to read more.

Familiarize Yourself with Multiple Platforms

Can you write 1,000 words in a day? Of course, you can. It's only two 500-word blogs. Those could be for your own site or posts you write on assignment. The point is to familiarize yourself with multiple writing formats. Just as different fiction genres require unique story structures, different web formats require different rules within those formats.

Many writers tend to have trouble blogging, and bloggers tend to have trouble writing. Master both, and you will be in high demand. Beyond that, learn how to craft catchy headlines to increase your hits (the number of people who click on your site).

One of the other key things to adapting the Jack-of-All-Trades principle is to recognize and embrace the many sources of digital distribution. Anyone trying to make a living in writing today must learn to distribute their writing through multiple platforms. Therefore, if you have a blog, challenge yourself by writing an ebook. If you're already an author, try crafting value-driven short social media posts to engage with and build your followers.

EXERCISE: Switch It Up:

What is your preferred writing format? Have you been working on a novel? Are you a blogger? A copywriter?

Choose a format as different as possible from your normal writing style. If you're a nonfiction writer, try fiction. If you're a fiction writer, try nonfiction.

Fiction: Write a one-page story outline. It doesn't matter what the story is, just sketch out the main character, the central conflict, and a brief overview of the action.

Nonfiction: Write a one-page sales letter with the goal of selling your writing services to a business. List compelling reasons why someone should hire you.

The goal is to get out of your comfort zone when it comes to writing styles and formats. Make time to try different writing styles to improve your skills.

A Final Thought on Audience Building

With the invention of the Internet, came a wealth of previously unavailable ways to distribute content. The old consequences still apply. If no one reads your writing, you are irrelevant. Even worse, you are most likely not being paid for writing.

The key to overcoming the irrelevancy hurdle is strategic and focused audience building. The reason why this is so crucial is with this endless content, there is a very real battle for eyeballs. Or readers. *Consumers*. The rules of the game may have changed, but the game itself hasn't. The objective is still the same: Readership = Fans = Loyalty. The prize for an active, engaged audience? Money.

In a later chapter, I will discuss how to build an audience. For now, keep its importance in mind along with the idea that content is king and you can have tremendous value as a content creator.

$ix-Figure Writer Tip: If you build an audience, you can monetize the audience quickly and consistently through your own branded content. If you build a highly trafficked blog, you can sell advertising space. If you build a loyal customer base of people buying your self-published book, you can write a follow-up and remarket to them.

Chapter Summary

- Technology has disrupted the traditional business model of writing distribution.
- It's the best time ever to be a writer since there are more opportunities for writers to earn a living thanks to digital media.
- Content is king and easily digestible, value-driven content is the key to success in the new digital Connection Economy.
- Writers have a competitive advantage in this new content-driven era because they are content creators who can produce large volumes of material on their own at no cost (except their own time and energy.)
- It's important to think of yourself as a business and not an artist in order to monetize your earning capabilities as a *$ix-Figure Writer*.
- Writers should be versatile and develop the ability to write in multiple formats as a Jack-of-All-Trades.
- Audience engagement needs to be a top priority.
- Familiarize yourself with multiple web platforms.
- Format your writing to meet and satisfy audience needs.
- Build an audience to ensure eyeballs on your work, an indicator of strong opportunities for monetization.

Action Steps:

- Integrate the new digital reality into your business.
- Take advantage of web-related platforms to increase your writing revenue.
- Content is king, so don't judge what others consider quality content. Position yourself to offer engaging material.
- Think of yourself as a content creation business and avoid the income-killing title of artist.
- Become a Jack-of-All-Trades to capitalize on numerous writing income streams.
- Concentrate on building an audience with the expectation of more eyeballs and more opportunity for monetization.

CHAPTER 3 -
CAN'T KNOCK THE HUSTLE

"The only thing that I see that is distinctly different about me is I'm not afraid to die on a treadmill. I will not be out-worked, period. You might have more talent than me, you might be smarter than me, you might be sexier than me, you might be all of those things you got it on me in nine categories. But if we get on the treadmill together, there's two things: You're getting off first, or I'm going to die. It's really that simple, right?

You're not going to out-work me. It's such a simple, basic concept. The guy who is willing to hustle the most is going to be the guy that just gets that loose ball. The majority of people who aren't getting the places they want or aren't achieving the things that they want in this business is strictly based on hustle. It's strictly based on being out-worked; it's strictly based on missing crucial opportunities. I say all the time if you stay ready, you ain't gotta get ready."

~Will Smith

Professional writing is a marathon, not a sprint. It requires practice and finesse to cross the finish line. This chapter covers the importance of "putting in your time" to develop strong writing habits and discipline.

Michael

Want to be a *$ix-Figure Writer*? Ask yourself these questions:

- Do you have good writing habits? If so, what are they? Do you wake up at four a.m. and write every day? Is it even important?
- Who is or what is your support system? Do you have beta readers? A critique group? Who reads your work to tell you if it's any good?
- What makes you special as a writer? What are your particular strengths?

Putting in Your Time

I won't admonish you to write every day. There are authors who swear by it, but I don't. However, I do advise you "put in your time." What do I mean by that?

In her book on creativity, *Big Magic,* Elizabeth Gilbert talks about developing her writing skillset. She employed a timer regimen. Gilbert committed to a certain number of hours before she could put her timer away and stop each day. She admits oftentimes none of the output was any good. Then again, some of it was fantastic. Beside the bestseller, *Eat, Pray Love,* she has published many other highly successful books.

What's more important than actual quality, however, is the habit. In the book, *Outliers,* author Malcolm Gladwell suggests to become proficient in any creative enterprise, from making music to programming to writing, you need 10,000 hours of practice. I subscribe to this idea and attribute my professional achievements to the significant amount of hours I put into practicing my craft.

A Screenwriting Incubator

After receiving my MFA, there was a period of five years when Charles Borg, my writing partner, and I wrote nearly every day. During that time, we churned out four original feature-length scripts, four original TV pilots, three specs for existing TV series, a three-season story bible for an animated series, and much other miscellaneous entertainment-related content.

My routine was to work an eight-hour workday at my insurance job, come home by 5:30 p.m. and then write until 9:30 p.m. every night.

Charles and I also wrote on the weekends. Frequently, we put in marathon sessions of ten-to-twelve hours of sustained screenwriting. On our meal breaks, we watched video clips of TV shows or movies for inspiration.

Over the course of that highly productive period, I estimate I logged more than 10,000 hours. I received a tremendous amount of practical experience. Through repetition, I developed expertise in crafting story ideas, sympathetic characters, and dramatic tension. From participating in countless meetings, I learned how to pitch story ideas in a succinct, but compelling narrative form.

If it weren't for that special time in my life, what I call my "Screenwriting Incubator," I wouldn't have been ready to take on the epic novel-writing project I embarked upon in Marin County. The disciplined writing habits I developed in my writing cocoon served me so well I could write for hours, day after day, even when I felt hopelessly overwhelmed by the manuscript's creative problems.

I relate this story because I am a huge proponent of "putting in your time" for your craft. Later, I'll discuss whether to participate in a professional educational program, but know this: it is not enough to go to school to learn the fundamentals. *You must do.*

$ix-Figure Writer Tip: Dispense with the idea you need to write every day. Instead, put in at least 10,000 hours (on your own schedule) to establish solid writing habits and discipline.

Good Writing is Informed by Good Reading

Culturally, we have preconceived notions as to how a writer behaves. Famous literary figures of the twentieth century, such as Norman Mailer, Jack Kerouac, Dorothy Parker, and James Joyce, come to mind. The typical stereotype is something like this: slaves to their work, these writers lived and worked hard, drank fiercely, savagely struggled and suffered to create their art.

Many misperceptions exist about the writer's lifestyle. Contrary to romantic fancies, most professional writers worth their salt don't drink while writing. But one thing today's aspiring writers could take from their notorious predecessors is often lost on many young people today: a fondness for the written word. Famous writers from the past were all in love with good writing.

Just as it is crucial to write over 10,000 words to hone your craft, it is essential to read everything.

$ix-Figure Writer Tip: Never be without a book or Kindle. Read anything and everything.

Don't Discriminate. Step Out of Your Comfort Zone

So are you an author who likes to write cozy, slow-burning mysteries set in the antebellum south? Great. Now go out and read mopey, French existentialist plays by Albert Camus. Find out why his work is still relevant. Read doorstop-sized nonfiction histories on the Middle Ages to understand how dead people once lived in faraway places hundreds of years ago.

Are you a liberal? Fine. Read Rush Limbaugh's political works to receive a contrary viewpoint.

Don't just stop at books. Read everything: blogs, essays, newspapers, and magazines. Devour comic books, political speeches, spiritual self-help columns, kinky erotica and speculative sci-fi anthologies.

Read it all. Read funny stuff and material only the other gender supposedly reads. When you're finished, delve into transgender fare. Read boring, technical manuals and obnoxious hate speech on bathroom stalls. Assume whatever you think you know about human behavior and patterns of speech is lacking. Fill in the blank spots with more content. Learn to inhabit minds unlike your own. Your goal of forays into far-out literary excursions is to bend your mind so profoundly you don't know if you'll ever come back.

After you've read everything I've suggested, find other content I haven't mentioned, like medical brochures and Shakespearean sonnets. Author Elizabeth George suggests before you sit down to write, read the very best in your genre to immerse yourself in the style and genre.

Do Your Homework: Get a Life

One of the best things about being a writer is the tremendous opportunity it affords you to learn about the world. Beyond reading everything in sight, you have another big assignment.

***$ix-Figure Writer* Tip**: Actually *live* your life.

Picture this: you've landed a dream assignment. *Sports Illustrated* loves your portfolio, so they've hired you to pen a series of articles on Extreme Sports. Your first topic: skydiving.

You have a problem. You've never jumped out of a plane. Nor have you bungee jumped. You've never even parasailed. How on earth are you going to write an article from a place of authenticity to convey what it feels like to skydive?

The only solution is: *live.*

As a writer, your role is to share experiences, stories, ideas, and characters convincingly with the world. It's your profession, and it's awesome. It's also an awesome responsibility. It requires you to have a plethora of real-world experiences.

Think you can fake it? Think again. I can't tell you how many students in my film school class produced vapid, trivial short films about Hollywood and the film industry because they had myopically spent their undergrad years studying only movies. They had experienced little outside their limited bubble, and it showed in the superficial work they produced.

This notion is even more vital when it comes to writing novels. Screenwriters can get away with creating pithy action scenes requiring little description, and no one will assume they really don't know what they're talking about. But if your hope is to transport readers to new, believable worlds with strong, descriptive prose, make your readers believe you are not a phony.

The best way to imbue your writing with verve and authenticity is to become a student of the world. Experience deep relationships. Fall in love. Break someone's heart. Have your own heart broken. Get into fights. Travel to exotic places. Eat weird foods. Get lost (a lot). Have sex.

Whether you wish to write blogs or web copy, you need to experience as much as you can. It's the best way to connect with your readers.

$ix-Figure Writer **Tip:** Share your work with people you respect and trust.

If Your Beta Reader Is Your Mom, You Have a Problem

Join a critique group. Right now. Go online to *Meetup* or find a church group. Not religious? Locate a school or work organization you like. Post a notice on Craigslist that you're starting your own. The point is you need eyeballs on your work.

The most common blunder I see among aspiring writers is they're afraid to share their work. Huge mistake. Let people critique you. You have to get your work to others who will tell you what you're doing right and wrong.

One important caveat: Make sure you are in a confident place first. You need to feel good enough about your writing so if you receive less than ecstatic positive feedback from others, it won't kill your dream.

A second caveat: Find the right group for you. It might take trying more than one to find a group with the kind of expertise you need. Aim for one with people who are already published. They have been through the application and rejection process and can provide guidance. Make sure they understand the genre you are writing.

In *On Writing*, Stephen King discusses the importance of feedback at length. He relates it to novel writing, but the metaphor extends to any kind of writing. King considers his first draft to be his "baby." The delicate baby must be protected and nourished until it is strong enough to receive the sometimes-harsh opinions of others. If your baby is so fragile it will fall apart upon the first negative feedback, it will kill the whole project, and whatever was potentially good about your manuscript will die a horrible death before its time.

Likewise, if you are a beginning writer, you must hone your craft and develop your capabilities to the point that if you get negative pointers, they won't hurt you so badly you give up.

EXERCISE: Use Beta Readers

Adopted from the tech world, the term "beta reader" refers to the (usually non-professional) person who

---

reads your material with the intent of giving you feedback to improve it. Here's how to get the most from these critical exchanges.

Step One: Determine you are in the correct mental and emotional place to share your work with others.

Step Two: Pick individuals outside your family to be your beta-readers. No lovers (or ex-lovers). Avoid friends. Why? All of these people have personal ties to you and are bound to give you compromised feedback.

Step Three: Once you have settled on the individual(s), send them your material with as little explanation as possible. You can describe the genre and its expectations but leave it at that. Your work should speak for itself. Give your readers a reasonable amount of time to read the work and provide you feedback.

Step Four: No matter what the beta readers tell you, good or bad, thank them. Be gracious, respectful, and appreciative of their time. Don't bother explaining yourself or defending your work. Absorb their feedback dispassionately with an aim toward professional improvement.

Step Five: One word of caution: be careful with other peoples' opinions. Remember, they are subjective and only opinions. You are the ultimate arbiter. Be willing to ignore others' advice if it conflicts with your own judgment. However, if more than two people give you the same critical note, give it serious attention.

Own Your Abilities

Recognize your strengths and weaknesses and embrace them. If you find you excel in blogging, but have trouble with narrative writing, don't be discouraged. If this were a creative-writing seminar, I'd suggest you keep practicing. One day you may get better.

This book is not light and fluffy that way. It's about helping you earn a six-figure income as a professional writer. Play to your strengths. Discover what you enjoy writing and develop those skills. Don't waste time doing hopelessly difficult assignments. Instead, use your time to market yourself.

Now you may be asking yourself, "What about all the practice you just talked about?" Practice your craft. Hone it. But remember, your first obligation is to write in a way that earns money. If you know novel writing is not your forte but churning out blogs is, by all means, spend those 10,000 hours improving your blogs.

Chapter Summary

- Contrary to popular exhortations to write every day, it is far better to commit at least 10,000 hours toward honing your craft. Focused practice will not only develop your skills, it will establish strong habits and good writing discipline.

- Quality writing is a result of reading across many genres and types. In order to be a consummate pro, a *$ix-Figure Writer* needs to expand his/her reading horizons.
- *$ix-Figure Writers* don't live in bubbles of isolation or ivory towers. They throw themselves into the messiness of life by having deep and diverse experiences. Good writing requires authenticity. Authenticity can be earned only through experiential living.
- Share your writing with others for their feedback. The best way to improve is to understand what is working—and what isn't. The best way to determine this for your own writing is to seek the opinions of others.
- Owning your strengths and weakness is paramount for a *$ix-Figure Writer.* It is not necessary to be a wizard at everything literary. Discover what you like to write and are good at. Then focus on earning a six-figure living through it.

Action Steps:

- Put lots of time into practicing your writing. Make it your goal to get to 10,000 hours to become an expert at your craft.
- Read anything and everything in sight to gain wider insight into other human beings and our world.
- Actively engage in life by having diverse and interesting experiences.

- Join a critique group of peers to give you candid feedback. Seek out beta readers (not emotionally related to you) for advice you can trust.
- Recognize what you write well, and go after that category to earn six figures.

CHAPTER 4 -
CONTENT IS KING

"Content is the only marketing left."

`Seth Godin

There has truly been a massive and profound shift in how we consume media. The last hundred years have seen our society go from print only to radio, television, and now the Internet. The web is arguably the biggest innovation in content distribution since the Gutenberg printing press.

As a people, we've become far more exposed to content and information. It's readily accessible everywhere we search. In fact, the average person now owns five screens: the TV, the desktop PC, the smart phone, the tablet, and the laptop. This chapter asks you to recognize a very simple, yet powerful observation. All our wonderful devices depend on one commodity: content.

If you embrace your immense value to provide that commodity through your unique services, you deserve to receive a six-figure income.

Societal Upheavals of the Information Age

Sham

The consumer Internet era began roughly in the mid-90s. Since then, there have also been a number of minor revolutions, the biggest being social media and the rise of mobile technology. Social media not only established the concept of self-identity online, it suddenly connected us in profound new ways. Online platforms, such as Facebook, Twitter, and Instagram, created new communication channels. Suddenly, we could all peer into the lives of our friends and family, along with celebrities and public figures.

The social media revolution was followed by the digital media revolution. New communication channels have made it easier for us to share and consume endless amounts of content. Increased Internet speed and improved technology have allowed us to consume more content in larger quantity. Finally, mobile devices, like smart phones and tablets, provide opportunity to access this content anywhere on demand.

Along with the increased ability to *consume* content came more efficient ways to create and distribute it. Just a few years ago, you needed an in-depth understanding of HTML to create a website. Now, with just a few mouse clicks, you can create your very own WordPress website and blog. Similarly, publishing used to be a long and arduous process requiring multiple edits, revisions, and formatting headaches. It could take months, if not years, between the submission of a manuscript to publication in bookstores, the only real way to sell mass quantities of books.

Not anymore.

A Generic Term

In this book, *content* is used as a generic term to refer to any form of digital material. A TV show has content. A blog post contains content. Websites convey important information. All of these fall under the category of content. Essentially, content is the fundamental component of all consumable media. It's the good stuff. The valuable material that all our fancy devices, from phones to flat screens, feature.

Someone has to create all the content to get those eyeballs watching. Someone like whom? You guessed it. *The $ix-Figure Writer.*

The Engine Behind Our Society

From the Internet to literature, to the TV shows and movies we watch, to the news we read, everything is made up of content. Content also drives practically everything we do online. When you post a selfie to Instagram, guess what? You're creating content. When you rant on someone's Facebook status, you're writing content. When you share a funny vine video, you`re distributing content. And when you`re binge watching a new show on Netflix you`re consuming content.

An Insatiable Demand Means Limitless Earning Potential

Do you want job security? How about providing the most widely consumed product in the world? That's what content is. As more societies acquire smart phone access, as data speeds increase, and digital media platforms grow, the demand will only increase for professionals who can provide this coveted resource.

It cannot be any clearer: content creators have exponential growth opportunities to satisfy an urgent need. Accept this as your invitation not only to do what you love, but reap the financial rewards of this digital revolution.

$ix-Figure Writer **Tip:** It's important to look at content in an analytical way. Start paying close attention to the type of content getting the most "likes" and shares on social media. Observe what kind of articles and videos are receiving the most distribution.

The Death Knell for Interruptive Advertising

According to strategic advisor, Rebecca Lieb, "Content that is too product or brand-focused does not travel well digitally, whereas content that stands on its own merits as entertainment, storytelling, or education and will be shared and passed along."

The digital media revolution has wrought an *advertising revolution* as well. It used to be simple back when everyone had one TV set and thirteen channels. You received content, such as the *I Love Lucy* show, in exchange for occasional interruptions in which companies advertised via commercials.

The model worked quite well for many years and still does occasionally. For example, most of us look forward to watching Super Bowl ads. It's a media event in and of itself. Exorbitantly expensive Super Bowl commercials possess a self-conscious relevance and inherent entertainment value consumers actively seek out. But what about the many businesses that can't afford to take advantage of such high-priced advertising?

Actually, they could take a cue from Super Bowl commercials' strong emphasis on entertainment-driven content. Because with so much readily available content, and so many options and choices as to when, where, and how to consume it, there is little need to passively accept the annoyance of interruptive advertising. Besides, traditional advertising is becoming less effective.

According to *Search Engine Land*, "80% of people ignore Google ads." *Arris* reports, "84% of TV viewers skip through commercials." and *Newscred* confirms that a whopping "44% of direct mail is never opened,"

We all know why. Traditional advertising is intrusive. It disrupts us. It *annoys* us. Consumers are fed up with it. Think about it. When was the last time you watched a full thirty-second ad on YouTube? Probably never. You skip through it. Beyond that, technological advances are also putting the preverbal nail in the advertising coffin. Ad blockers inoculate consumers from having to sit through ads.

Brands as Publishers

Remember the recent *Old Spice* campaign, "The Man Your Man Could Smell Like"? It was an Internet sensation, a cultural phenomenon, which generated huge word of mouth buzz and even copycat celebrity fan references. How about the quirky genius of the "Stay Thirsty" campaign from *Dos Equis*? People love those commercials and will actually sit through them when they come on. These are two effective examples of brands acting as publishers.

Branded content is content which offers value or engagement with a company's target audience. It is published and distributed under a company's brand name. The idea of brands acting of publishers is the new paradigm for marketing in this digital media revolution.

Forward-thinking executives have understood this for years. Even formerly stalwart holdouts are finally waking up and smelling the coffee. Savvy companies are rushing to leverage content in order to market themselves to consumers. They realize the immense advantage of having a well-thought-out content strategy. Brands are investing big dollars in providing the best content possible. It's a simple formula as exemplified by the above examples. Create content and leverage it to reach more followers to grow your audience. Then retain your audience by providing them more and more enjoyable content. You will build trust as a source for value-driven entertainment consistently and regularly. (And of course, manage to deliver your message.)

Take Advantage of Content-Driven Marketing

A powerful and effective way to capitalize on your writing abilities is to focus on content creation, whether through your own brand, or by charging to create it for others. Consider the campaigns I just mentioned. Can you imagine how much the writers were paid to generate those ads?

Even if you never make it to the big leagues providing branded content to big corporations, you can still market yourself to smaller businesses, which see the need for this service. Huge opportunities exist for writers who can leverage storytelling to craft engaging content. By correctly positioning yourself as a content creator who fully understands the content-driven marketing approach, you will find yourself in high demand.

$ix-Figure Writer Tip: You can also apply the *Brands as Publishers* approach to your own writing and market yourself through engaging self-branding.

Your Own Content On Demand

It used to be prohibitively expensive to self-publish. Today, however, you can write a manuscript and hire a freelance editor to revise and format your book inexpensively. You can also outsource a freelance designer to make a beautiful, eye-grabbing cover. After that, press a few buttons to quickly upload your baby onto Amazon KDP or Kobo or MOBI, and presto, you're ready to sell it yourself as an ebook. In addition, not only can you sell it in digital format, but through Amazon's CreateSpace service, you can print your book on demand for anyone interested in acquiring a physical copy. We did it, and you're looking at the proof.

It all goes back to the New Reality discussed in Chapter 2: there are no gatekeepers anymore. But also recall another point: there is no guarantee your work won't disappear into irrelevance after self-publishing. Your potential book sales hinge on you and your ability to build an audience. The key is the ease in creating and distributing your own content based on the web's power of reach. In particular, the digital media revolution has given writers a massive advantage. Our new ability to publish and distribute content is truly revolutionary.

The New Era of Thought Leadership

The term, Thought Leader, is one of those cool, buzz-wordy titles people like to drop to sound trendy and innovative. It describes anyone viewed as an authority figure or expert on a specific topic. Thought Leaders are sought after for their knowledge and opinions. But there is one fundamental difference between a Thought Leader and a traditional expert. Thought Leaders are not only authorities on a topic or industry. They also offer new ideas and innovations.

As writers, we have the opportunity to build a following from our content. Position yourself not only as a writer or content creator, but as a *Thought Leader* in your given area of expertise. You stand to earn considerable revenue from multiple streams, such as ebooks, advertising income from your platform(s), and even speaking engagements.

The first step is to brand yourself. Examples of superb writers who have mastered this include Danielle LaPorte for personal development based on consciousness and Joanna Goddard for women's lifestyle blogging. Both of these highly successful Thought Leaders are killing it when it comes to self-branding. They have managed to exploit diverse revenue streams based on their devoted followers who view them as authorities in their respective fields.

The wonderful thing for you as a *$ix-Figure Writer* is people are hungry for content to allow them to discover new ideas and learn. Let the reach of the web, and in particular social media, propel your expertise to others eager for valuable information. This niche promises untold riches for individuals who can find the right balance between useful knowledge and effective branding.

How It's Done

Consistency of content is critical to build your authority properly. This may be achieved through a steady stream of branded ebooks, blogs, articles, podcasts, and/or videos. The mechanism of choice (or combination thereof) is not nearly as important as the aspect of consistency. Consistent content not only builds momentum, it generates trust from your audience while growing it. Simply deciding to call yourself a Thought Leader and expecting people to come to you won`t achieve your goals. You need to be highly proactive on a consistent basis with leveraged content to provide value to your followers.

One of the main reasons I was able to build such a large following for my online vape publication quickly was consistency. I knew I wasn't the first to blog about the vape industry. In fact, four other major blog sites, as well as three physical magazines, were already covering the same topic. In addition, these entities had been in operation for at least a year before I began. Nevertheless, my company built a bigger online following within six months and a wider readership base.

How? Consistency. Consistency. Consistency. My organization put out two, sometimes three original articles every day. When we started building our UK/Europe readership, we pumped out even more, timing the posting for daylight hours across the globe. An important caveat: consistency creates momentum to drive you forward, but it requires front-loaded, initial legwork. It is much easier to go from 15,000 followers to 20,000 than it is to go from zero to 1,000.

EXERCISE: Become a Thought Leader Today

STEP ONE: Determine a subject or field you can confidently describe yourself as an expert in. (Don`t worry if it's obscure or involves a small niche. You would be surprised how passionate a devoted following can be about a seemingly minor pursuit. Besides, you need to position yourself as an authority on something you understand and possess a strong knowledge base about.)

STEP TWO: Once you have determined the above, write down three big ideas regarding that field of knowledge.

STEP THREE: Next to each one, list one unique idea you have to improve your niche. (Don't worry about being criticized. If you want to be perceived as a Thought Leader, you must be willing to submit your original ideas to the public for their input.)

STEP FOUR: Start churning out content. Consistently.

STEP FIVE: Build an audience by actively engaging online through social media platforms on a consistent basis.

Bring on the Haters

Thought Leadership requires appealing to both the intellectual and emotional in others. You need to appeal to your audience's rational side by presenting interesting, innovative ideas aimed at transcending a given school of thought or expertise. But that's only half the equation. You also need to appeal to people's emotional nature by inspiring them to follow you and believe in your ideas. Either one of these appeals can generate strong reactions.

Accept that being a Thought Leader involves negative as well as positive feedback. Though you obviously want people to agree with you and like the content you provide, detractors can provide value to your platform. Remember the saying, "There's no such thing as bad publicity"? It applies here.

The price you pay for positioning yourself as an expert is critical feedback. Yes, you will always have haters. But it's not such a bad thing. It generates more discussion, more engagement. Focus on the people who agree with you and leverage them to share and distribute your ideas. But don't worry about the opposition. In some ways, they are actually doing you a big favor.

$ix-Figure Writer **Tip:** When building a following for your content, organic reach is always better than paid, but don't stop experimenting with paid ads. They can increase the exposure of a particular social media post to give you an extra edge.

Chapter Summary

- Consumption of written content is now dominated by the Internet in unprecedented ways.
- Social media provides multiple distribution channels to get eyeballs on your content.
- Today's writers have enormous potential to build following and establish audiences for their content through the web's tremendous reach.
- Content is a supreme commodity, the good stuff people read or watch, whether online or offline.
- The exponential increase in demand for content provides writers a seemingly limitless opportunity to earn income. Writers are in huge demand because they provide the most widely consumed product in the world: content.
- Traditional, interruptive advertising is quickly becoming irrelevant as consumers gravitate toward entertaining or educational marketing, which meaningfully engages audiences.
- Content Marketing is the new preferred paradigm for companies wishing to promote their businesses and build their brands. Consequently, huge opportunities exist for writers and storytellers to create content.
- Brands must now think like publishers as traditional methods of marketing have lost their previous effectiveness.
- With the advent of the Internet, self-publishing is now a viable and economical option for writers wishing to sell their content.

- Thought Leadership provides writers a great opportunity to establish themselves as leading experts in their chosen field of expertise.

Action Steps:

- Follow and read leading digital media platforms, such as *Buzzfeed*, *The Huffington Post*, *Salon*, and *Vice*. Pay attention to how they craft original content and their consistent output.
- Practice writing short, value-driven content pieces to replicate material you observe on the big content platforms.
- Formulate ideas for potential ebooks you could write and self-publish for an additional revenue stream.
- Determine an industry or subject in which you can be perceived as a Thought Leader.
- Build your Thought Leader brand through consistent quality content.
- Stay current with the latest news about what other Thought Leaders in your chosen niche are doing, but also put effort into developing your own ideas.

CHAPTER 5 -
TWO PATHS TO EARNING SIX FIGURES

"Perfecting and selling your writing is a lifelong task. If you are a persistent writer, you can expect your abilities to improve with time. Success is the ability to go from failure to failure without losing your enthusiasm."

~Winston Churchill

There are two ways to earn money as a *$ix-Figure Writer:* selling your services and/or selling your writing. Both have merit for different reasons. Both can help you accomplish your financial goals. This chapter explores each path in detail to provide you with valuable information about how to best monetize your craft.

PATH #1: SELLING YOUR SERVICES

The Connection Economy is Your Friend

Michael

In olden times, a metalsmith might spend years honing his craft, apprenticing with a mentor before striking out on his own to secure commissions. Today's working craftspeople must engage in a similar pursuit. We have the good fortune of living in the post-industrial age, a financial era, which marketing guru, Seth Godin, calls The Connection Economy.

The metalsmith is a bygone relic. In modern times, we rely on huge corporate entities for our metal needs. Similarly, the need for other artisans specializing in physical crafts has diminished. Interestingly though, what has replaced the physical artisan is the *immaterial artisan,* a professional who deals with non-physical entities, such as ideas and information. Enter the writer. At a time when the world is overflowing with relatively inexpensive physical commodities, a most valuable resource is the person who can manipulate the immaterial: written content.

Chapter 1 mentioned how the writer's mind cannot be replaced, but it bears repeating here. Writers have another advantage in the current market to sell their services. Unlike physical commodities, quality original content is in short supply.

As a writer, if you can position yourself to make use of the current demand for your services, you can command a significant income. In the next chapter, we will delve into some of the major service-related writing categories, such as blogging, copywriting, and journalism. For now, recognize the huge demand for wordsmiths or writers for hire. Just like the bygone metalsmith, think of yourself as a kind of literary artisan and position yourself for the most lucrative need.

Wordsmiths for Hire vs. Freelancers

At the time of this publication, I currently manage a writing services company with my fellow writer and wife. Full disclosure: it was her idea to work for ourselves as freelancers. I can't take credit. I'll come back to the story, but first, the last term bears clarification. Depending upon your social circle, the term *freelancer* can signify either romantic, creative freedom or abject poverty interrupted with unpredictable inflows of recompense.

When establishing our writing company, my wife and I were wary about being labeled freelancers. We covered the strategic need for the correct perception in Chapter 1, so you can understand our concern. Freelancing is associated with both infrequent payment and opportunity. Operating a small business as entrepreneurs has legitimate value. Freelancing indicates fly-by-night opportunities. Operating a business suggests permanence, profits, and security. Which label would you choose to define your career?

Back to our company's story. Here's how it all came about. After completing the novel I was commissioned to write for a year, I flirted with the idea of reentering the workforce as a copywriter. (I'm under contract for a whole series, but I needed income while I waited for the first book to be published.)

As I completed resumes on Monster.com and checked Craigslist for job postings, my heart sank. It's hard to get a job in this economy. It's even harder to get a respectable W-2 job with benefits as a writer. If you're lucky, a company will pay you peanuts for three-to-five years before ever considering raising your salary.

As I mentioned before, I have a background in finance and sales, so I even considered taking a job in one of those industries while writing on the side.

Then my wife had an epiphany. "Let's open our own writing company," she suggested. "We can work for ourselves." Both of us had contacts from our days as freelance copywriters and Hollywood connections from freelance screenwriting. If we leveraged them, we could replace the middlemen, who usually secured us those jobs, and keep all the money for ourselves. Thus began our foray into the wordsmithing business, providing writing services for hire, mostly for small business owners.

Six-Figure Writer **Tip:** Don't call yourself a freelance writer. Start your own writing business and brand to create a professional, successful perception.

Establish Your Pipeline

I could say my wife and I own a writing business even if we had no clients in reality. So let's not put too much stock into the image we project. It is, after all, only a perception. Since we are steadily adding to our knowledge base, it's time we move beyond the simple idea of what you appear to be and on to what you are.

"Fake it 'til you make it" is a good plan at the outset, but it is not sustainable. In the beginning of your writing career, you need to project a successful persona. You don't want people to believe you live in your parents' basement. The main reason for this is they will pay you accordingly. But now, it's time to grow up. It's time to position your own writing company and begin acquiring clients. The most effective way to do that is through the *Pipeline Approach.*

As I mentioned, I used to work as a mortgage broker on commission. Every loan I closed was a discrete one-time-only occurrence. There were no repeat deals. Consequently, I couldn't afford *not* to build my potential customer base while servicing my current clients. You want to think the same way in terms of your writing business. Build yourself a working pipeline. Always have another project or client on deck.

Six-Figure Writer **Tip:** Begin the preliminary work for your next project while you are still working on the current one to ensure you are never without steady income.

The Perpetual Need for Writing Services

This is the key to Path #1. Every business has writing needs, but most people can't write. Also, most business owners are too busy running their business to create the quality writing they need.

Memorize that last paragraph. Let it flow through your veins like the blood that sustains you. This is the value proposition you give to all potential clients. They need you. It's important enough to repeat again. *They. Need. You.*

What I do I mean? Let's imagine you are lawyer. How can you distinguish yourself from the hundreds or thousands of other lawyers who live in your area and constitute your competition (not to mention big law firms, nationals, or even internationals)? One good way is to have a well-written blog in which you *educate* people (*free*) about the services you provide. Emphasis on these words: *free* and *educate.*

When potential clients Google lawyers in your zip code, your blog will show up. You just gained an edge on your competitors. If I need a lawyer specializing in mechanic liens but can't tell the difference between lawyer A and lawyer B, reading a well-written blog by lawyer A, which demonstrates competence, knowledge, and expertise, will go a long way toward convincing me I should obtain his or her services over lawyer B.

The Case for a Ghostwriter

Blogs are helpful for business owners, but what's even better is a well-written book to establish credibility. If you're a typical lawyer putting in sixty or more hour workweeks, it's doubtful you have the time or stamina to pump out a two-hundred-page book to be used as your twenty-first century business card. So what do you do?

Easy. You employ a *ghostwriter* to pen the book and self-publish it through a platform such as CreateSpace. This is where the *$ix-Figure Writer* comes in. It's your opportunity to earn a great deal of money for a much-needed product and service.

Now expand this concept to encompass not just the legal profession, but all kinds of vocations: chiropractors, dentists, fitness instructors, the list goes on and on. Are you beginning to see why writers are in such demand? If you scale it right, you could easily be earning a six-figure income just by tapping all the needy professionals in your immediate vicinity who recognize the value of top-notch writing to educate and convert their customers.

The Case for Other Types of Writing

Beyond blogs and the ghostwritten book, there are so many avenues for written deliverables you can provide clients if you convince them you are the right person for the job. In the next chapter, we will go through these in depth, but consider these categories: web copy, newsletters, resumes, PowerPoint presentations, commercials, email blasts, internal memos, speeches, etc.

As a *$ix-Figure Writer* in demand, you could be the one providing all of these.

EXERCISE: **Transcend the Perception of Being a Successful Writer by Becoming One**

STEP ONE: Think of your writing as a craft to be sold as a service or commodity.

STEP TWO: Position yourself as a writer for hire (or wordsmith) by providing writing services on demand for clients.

STEP THREE: Eschew the lackluster label of freelancer. Instead, position your brand by establishing your own writing services company.

STEP FOUR: As you begin acquiring clients, always be on the hunt for more to add to your existing pipeline.

A Final Word on Wordsmithing

Wordsmith is a term I previously associated with the Bard or the nebbish curator of a collegiate poetry quarterly. In recent years though, I have actually come to embrace it as a viable brand. The transformation occurred after my copywriting mentor referred to me as one during a conference call with clients. "You can trust Michael with all your writing needs," said Chris. "He's our wordsmith on retainer."

I considered the idea and embraced it. Here's why: lots of people think they can write, but can't. If you tell people you are a writer, especially if you have an MFA in writing, people will often ask you to review their work for content or grammar. In these situations, a wordsmith provides expert feedback, much like a craftsman might advise you on how to build your home. Embrace the title of wordsmith, and you'll engender the trust of others who may return to you when they need help creating more content. By gaining their trust through providing solid advice and helpful feedback, you will have earned the opportunity to work with them again. Most importantly, you've opened the door for them to pay you.

The Importance of Trust

Let there be no confusion on this last point because it leads to the great *$ix-Figure Writer Axiom*.

Building trust as someone's wordsmith is just one example of what you need to do constantly as a professional writer. Besides talent or discipline, no greater factor determines the potential success of a writer than the ability to generate trust with clients.

It's essential. Every phone call, every scheduled appointment, each deadline for deliverables, each creative meeting, every single word or interaction is a chance to do one of one of two things: either build trust or erode trust. *Always* err on the side of building trust. It is the cornerstone of earning a six-figure income as a professional writer.

> **$ix-Figure Writer Axiom:** Every interaction with a client (or future client) is a chance to do one of two things: build trust or erode trust.

PATH #2: SELLING YOUR WRITING

Generally, when people think of writers, they think of them in terms this path. The romantic stereotype of the perfectionist slaving over a manuscript fits the notion of a writer who sells his or her own creative vision.

The industry term for this type of original content is *on spec,* meaning "on speculation." For instance, a freelancer may write an article on spec with the hope a magazine will buy it and publish it. It's a gamble, though. When you write on spec, you hope what you write will be so compelling it will have commercial merit and earn you money.

For many writers, Path #2 is the *only* path. It promises notoriety and glory. When aspiring writers first read revered novelists, like Philip Roth or Margaret Atwood, and then dream of one day having their own distinguished writing career, they envision themselves creating a book they'll sell to a publisher.

There are many challenges to this familiar model, however. The first is the actual writing. Writing a book is hard. Most people have no idea how hard until they actually try it. Many people (myself included at one point) have been deluded into thinking how simple it must be to write a book after reading so many in their lifetime. One reason is good writing *appears* effortless. A good writer makes his or her words flow off the page as simply as you and I talk. What is not readily apparent to the novice is the sheer amount of critical thought required for those beautifully executed pages.

However, the thoughts don't always come from just *one* mind. Often books are not written alone. Nearly every writer has a critique group or partner to receive feedback. Beta readers give the writer comments. Beyond that, every successful book requires a skillful editor, who works with the writer to ensure the final product is in top shape before it's sent to market. The point is writing doesn't occur in a vacuum, nor is it as simple as putting marks on a page. It requires years and years of dedication, hard work, intelligence, and creativity to churn out good material.

Beyond the challenges of writing a book is the equally difficult *if not more* challenging problem of getting a book published. If you are a screenwriter, the problem is analogous to getting your screenplay bought or produced. Even if you have a good piece of original work, there is no guarantee you'll ever sell it unless you make the right connections. This means getting your stuff to the decision-makers: the agents, editors, publishers, etc. who will make one crucial determination: will this content make us money?

Will They Decide You're the Prettiest Girl at the Ball?

Remember how it felt at the school dance waiting for someone to pick you? (Guys who have not had this experience can liken it to the stress of being picked for team sports.) In either instance, the situation can be hard on one's self-esteem. Not getting picked can make you feel unworthy, unattractive, or useless. No one likes feeling powerless. It's terrible being at the mercy of someone else for validation.

The gut-wrenching game of selling your writing is similar to the emotional rollercoaster of hoping to be picked. If you didn't like being at the mercy of someone selecting you for something as trivial as the baseball team or the school dance, try compounding the uncertainty with bigger stakes, such as your time, your blood, sweat, and tears.

Anyone who has spent hours crafting their writing and then submitting it to decision-makers for their response is all too aware of the agony of waiting. It's harrowing to be subject to the whims of another human. If a decision-maker declines your query (or worse, ignores it) you stand to lose much more than face. You lose your time, which equates to money.

This leads to some important questions. Do you like to gamble? Are you willing to roll the dice that your hard work and time will pay off? That it will be liked by others and therefore legitimized so you can earn money? Are you willing to let others pick you?

> **$ix-Figure Writer Tip:** Don't wait for decision-makers to pick you. Pick yourself.

Life Hacking: Reverse the Power Dynamic

Pre-Internet, writers were at the mercy of decision-makers, such as publishers, editors, and agents. It was tough to break out, especially if you didn't know the right person. Luckily, the antiquated power structure is dying. Post-Internet, you don't have to wait for someone else's permission. You don't have to give your power away. You can self-publish and earn all the net profits for yourself. If you're a screenwriter, you can create your own movies or web-series for a fraction of what it used to cost to produce.

The beauty of picking yourself in this brave new model is the old guard doesn't have a monopoly on distribution either. Using the Internet, it's possible to disseminate your work to the entire world. The downside, of course, is just because you self-published a book or created a video based on your screenwriting, it doesn't mean anyone cares. It's up to you to create a platform or buzz to get eyeballs on your work. Please refer to Sham's advice in Chapter 12 for information on how to build your own platform.

An Important Caveat

In spite of the difficulty of getting your writing picked, it's wonderful when it happens. Having a traditionally published book is a big deal. More than anything, it gives you credibility. What it signals to the public is this: some people think highly enough about my writing they were willing to take the risk of marketing and publishing me.

If Harper Collins publishes your novel or the *New Yorker* publishes your short story, it's incredibly validating and helpful for your earning prospects. (Not to mention your self-esteem.) Being traditionally published can open doors for your career. It gives you leverage, demonstrating to clients and future clients that you are a professional writer. But most of all, being traditionally published can lead to money. This leads us to Path #3.

PATH #3 The *$ix-Figure Writer*'s Way

Part life hack, part creative pragmatism, the best advice I can give is to merge Paths #1 and #2 to ensure your success as a *$ix-Figure Writer*. Seek out conventional publishing for name recognition. Then parlay your credibility into other avenues you control.

(By the way, if you are one of the elite few, such as J.K. Rowling, who can earn an abundant living strictly via Path #2, good for you. You represent a special minority, and I applaud your success. For the rest of us workaday types, I advise Path #3 for long-term, consistent income.)

For instance, I gained credibility from selling a movie treatment to Disney. This win opened the door for me to take on more writing services assignments (Path #1). One of those was a commission to write a middle-grade novel. A conventional publisher is currently reading it. Most likely, the book will be traditionally published (Path #2) in the next year. It would be wonderful, but I won't hold my breath until it happens. And I certainly won't wait for the so-called decision-makers to determine how I earn my income from writing in the meantime.

As you know, Sham and I self-published this book. We intend to take full advantage of both paths to optimize our reach and earning potential. This is the model I recommend. Like any good financial advisor would say, "Diversify." The best approach for the *$ix-Figure Writer* is not one path, but a combination of both at different times for greatest financial optimization.

Chapter Summary

- There are two paths to monetizing writing as a *$ix-Figure Writer*: selling your services or selling your writing.
- Selling your services entails taking on writing assignments from clients, such as being paid to write an industry blog.
- Selling your writing is the more traditional approach and usually entails making a sale on spec, to another entity, such as a publisher.
- The Connection Economy is an advantageous marketplace for today's writers because of the high demand for creative content. Like a physical artisan of days past, a *$ix-Figure Writer* can command a sizable income through writing commissions.

- Establishing a pipeline of revolving clients is the key to success as a *$ix-Figure Writer.* The more projects or clients on deck, the better you can ensure consistent, steady income.
- Use the term wordsmith to build your brand as a trusted expert on all things writing-related.
- The *$ix-Figure Writer Axiom* states: "Every interaction with a client (or future client) is a chance to do one of two things: build trust or erode trust."
- Path #2 can be problematic for many writers because of the powerless dynamic involved. Waiting for a decision-maker to pick you may take a long time and/or never happen. It is far better to be proactive and pick yourself.
- The ideal path for a *$ix-Figure Writer* is to combine both paths into Path #3. Path #3 parlays the credibility of selling your writing to a traditional entity, such as a publisher, with the entrepreneurial approach of Path #1 for maximum success.

Action Steps:

- Avoid calling yourself a freelancer. Choose to establish your own writing business for maximum credibility (and tax purposes).
- Seek out clients (predominantly small-business owners) who have need for writing services.

- Embrace the pipeline model by constantly having the next client or project on deck.
- Fully embrace the *$ix-Figure Writer Axiom:* every interaction between you and a client is a chance to establish trust.
- Seek out traditional opportunities to sell your writing. However, if they are not forthcoming, pick yourself.
- Combine the best features of both Path #1 and Path #2 in Path #3 to be truly successful as a *$ix-Figure Writer.* Attempt to receive credibility through traditional decision-makers, such as publishers, but don't let it be your only source of income. Trade on credibility to leverage your personal brand and optimize your income.

CHAPTER 6 - DIFFERENT TYPES OF WRITING YOU CAN SELL

"But words are things, and a small drop of ink, falling like dew upon a thought, produces that which makes thousands, perhaps millions, think."

~Lord Byron, *Don Juan*

Building upon the information contained in the last chapter on selling your services, this chapter seeks to break down the various types of writing you can sell. It offers specific, actionable information based on defined writing categories.

For each writing category, there are three components:

- An overview
- What is expected
- The advantages and disadvantages of writing this item for pay

COPYWRITING

Overview:

Michael

Quick Sprout defines copywriting as, "The art and science of writing copy (words used on web pages, ads, promotional materials, etc.) that sells your product or service and convinces prospective customers to take action."

If you are familiar with the TV show, *Mad Men,* you've probably seen Don and Peggy deliberating for hours on just the right turn of phrase to promote companies, such as Mohawk Airlines or Dow Chemical. Traditional corporate marketing departments of the past put a strong emphasis on compelling ad copy via brochures, commercials, magazine spreads, and billboards to sell their products. Today, a lot of the effort has been diverted into modern platforms, such as web copy, videos, and social media posts. Copywriting can take many forms, but the basic idea is to generate powerful words, which concisely and effectively convey a client's brand in order to convert sales.

What is Expected:

Creating good copywriting is all about two things: clarity and knowledge.

Clarity: No one wants to read a long ad. If your reader becomes aware they are reading copy, they will tune out.

Short, pithy sentences, which stick in the mind, work best. "Snickers really satisfies you" is ideal copy. It's quick and snappy. Most of all, it's memorable, providing instant brand recognition.

Knowledge: As a copywriter, it's not enough to know your product or service inside and out. (Although it's a must.) You also need *uncommon* knowledge. What do I mean? Returning to Chapter 2, I advised you to both read and live.

You need to do both to obtain a kind of intangible awareness about ideas, things, and most of all, *people*. You need to know what they care about. What they think about. You need to know pop culture and historical references. This is a tall order, but learn as much as possible about as many different things as possible to create good copy. Why? The more you know, the more opportunities you have to use your knowledge in creative, unusual ways.

Advantages and Disadvantages of Copywriting for Pay:

Advantage: Copywriting is always in demand and can pay well.

Advantage: Higher education is not a requirement to copy write. No MFAs needed here.

Advantage: As opposed to long-term projects, like books, copywriting can be written quickly, freeing you to take on more projects.

Disadvantage: Copywriting can be tedious, dull, and uninspiring.

Disadvantage: Many companies hire copywriters for little pay at the outset and require you to work for them as an employee.

Disadvantage: Clients often think they know how to write their own copy better than you, leading to creative arguments, annoyance and frustration.

BLOGGING

Overview:

Initially written off as a pastime for the self-absorbed or the perpetually lonely, this medium has blossomed into a lucrative enterprise in recent years. Pick up any popular magazine, and you will see most of the traditional space for text has been replaced by images. Much of the world's exceptional writing no longer exists in print form because publishers know their audience has changed its reading habits. Print is dying.

Today, engaged readers (especially younger ones) seek out content online through digital blogs found on sites such as *Buzzfeed, Medium, Salon,* and the *Huffington Post.* In addition, many forward-thinking business owners are wisely utilizing blogging's immense power to grow their site's traffic.

Why? Generally, blogs are short (approximately 400 to 500 words is a good range). They contain easily digestible content. Oftentimes blogs are hyperlinked to *other blogs,* which contain information of similar interest. As mentioned, blogs may also be used by business owners, such as the lawyer who sets himself apart from his competition by blogging to demonstrate his expertise, thus converting eyeballs into sales.

What is Expected:

Most blogs are short. They tend to encompass one topic with a few supportive paragraphs. Often, pictures accompany text. Simpler blogs can be created, such as a listicle, an article presented in the form of a numbered or bullet-pointed list like you might find on *Buzzfeed*. An example: "Top 5 Signs You Are on Your Way to Becoming a *$ix-Figure Writer*." Major traits expected of a blogger include an authentic voice and the ability to organize short pieces around an easily identifiable theme.

Advantages and Disadvantages of Writing Blogs for Pay:

Advantage: Blogs can be created without too much general knowledge on any given subject.

Advantage: If specific knowledge is required, it can be easily Googled within a matter of seconds, establishing credibility.

Advantage: Blogs can be written speedily without much fuss.

Disadvantage: A stigma remains that bloggers are not "real writers."

Disadvantage: Business owners are loath to pay big bucks for blogs.

Disadvantage: When building a portfolio, blogs are not as prestigious as some literary items because they exist on the web, not in print.

SOCIAL MEDIA

Overview:

From Facebook posts to Tweets, social media writing can mean many different things. Even blogs could be lumped into this category. Perhaps the defining feature of social media over other writing types is its principal focus on *interaction*. People can comment upon your posts, repost them, "like" them, add to the conversation, etc.

You may notice an overlap between social media writing and other types of online writing. For instance, you can also comment on people's blogs and articles. For that reason, strict social media as used in this book means anything shorter than a blog written for someone else to interact digitally.

Social media posts tend to be written in conversational style and can be highly effective for audience building to create loyalty and brand devotion. You can be paid to engage in written conversations via social media platforms. For instance, my colleague was once hired to manage a well-known celebrity's charity website as their "social media liaison." The celebrity was so popular his Facebook inbox was slammed with 200-300 emails a day, not to mention how many people populated his wall with personal messages. There was no way this person could possibly respond to all of these message every day, even if he wanted to.

To earn her hourly rate, my colleague was expected to interact socially with each of these people in the celebrity's voice. She was paid to write individualized messages to make them feel welcome and special. Since it was a charity for people suffering through difficult times, she was often called upon to counsel those who wrote by providing emotional support and compassion. A significant reason she was compensated so well was because the people who wrote in described highly intimate, personal things, which required the human touch, sensitivity, and considerable thought.

What is Expected:

As opposed to blogs or copywriting ads, which might be discrete one-offs, social media writing can feel endless. The writing could go on forever so long as there are people who continue to respond. That could be a good thing if you are paid hourly. However, if you are the kind of person who thrives on closure, social media's open-ended aspect could drive you nuts. Last, like blogging, since social media is so casual, there is little need for a formal writing education to be successful.

Advantages and Disadvantages of Writing Social Media for Pay:

Advantage: Requires very little knowledge, research or formal writing training.

Advantage: An ongoing social media hourly rate can provide a continual revenue stream.

Advantage: Many business owners will happily outsource this activity to avoid the time involvement.

Disadvantage: Unless you are being paid by the hour, the large time commitment can be frustrating.

Disadvantage: Social media writers tend to be paid less than bloggers and receive less respect for their efforts.

Disadvantage: It can be hard to generate fresh post ideas consistently in order to build an active following.

JOURNALISM

Overview:

In the past, this position paid decently and even offered benefits. Today, only celebrity writers with the *New York Times*, like Paul Krugman, can earn a comfortable living on a journalist's pay. To be fair, reporter jobs still exist, but the pay is dismal, and the job security is nonexistent.

Many struggling journalists have accepted this new reality and have turned to freelance print/online journalism assignments to make ends meet. I myself did this for a year. It paid okay. I earned $300 for a 1,000-word article that took three hours to write (on average). So I made about $100/hour. Not bad. But then again, my editor only wanted one such article *a month.* Now do you see why freelancing isn't the best option?

The reality these days is many "journalists" are paid to be glorified ad people. The articles they write have little relation to journalistic objectivity (if such a thing still exists.) As a so-called journalist, you may be expected to write in a "fair and balanced" tone. However, your writing will often be used to push someone else's business platform.

What is Expected:

Be prepared to abandon the pretense of journalistic objectivity when you freelance as a journalist. Many times, you are hired simply to promote an agenda. The better you are at generating compelling propaganda, the better you will fare.

Please don't mistake my candor for condescension. I am past the point of being offended by what is asked of me as a writer. You would do well to follow my example. To be a *$ix-Figure Writer,* you will be asked to write things which might conflict with your sensibilities. You may think it is noble to hold onto your beliefs and refuse such assignments. It is unimportant to me what position you take on this issue. My purpose is only to tell you how to maximize your profits by being pragmatic. If you realize your beliefs are too strong to write about something you are opposed to, I suggest you opt out. I quit being a journalist when my conscience could no longer abide the items I was expected to write about.

Advantages and Disadvantages of Journalism for Pay:

Advantage: Journalists often receive the prestige of writing for a well-respected medium.

Advantage: It is easier to parlay a journalistic portfolio into many better-paying writing careers, such as speechwriting or writing fulltime as an author.

Advantage: You can (typically) expect higher pay than being a blogger or social media writer.

Disadvantage: Journalists are expected to do more research than the other writing types so far discussed.

Disadvantage: It can be harder to acquire journalistic jobs than other new media writing gigs and may require a college degree.

Disadvantage: Journalists may be expected to work long hours and still not receive benefits. Freelancing gigs can be inconsistent.

GHOSTWRITING

Overview:

Per the current estimate, over 80% of books are ghostwritten. It may sound like a shocking figure to you.

It was to me until I witnessed firsthand how hard it is to write a book.

However, it's crucial for today's small business owners to differentiate themselves from their competition by self-publishing. Think back to the small business owners you know. Can you imagine them sitting down and crafting a polished book to convey their brand effectively? Even if they had the writing ability, can you imagine them finding the time to write such a thing?

This is where you come in. There is a *huge* need for ghostwriting today, especially since it's so easy to self-publish. Beyond the small business owner, numerous other clients, such as celebrities or politicians, need their own book for any number of reasons: to promote themselves, to stay relevant, to appear as an expert in their field. If you position yourself correctly, you can obtain these lucrative assignments.

Another possible area for ghostwriting is the creative collaborator. Many people have book ideas. Most of them put off the idea of writing because they lack the proper training. If you meet these people, (see the next chapter on networking for more about this) you will have a unique opportunity to help them achieve their goals.

What is Expected:

Some writers may have a problem with this type of writing because it's the antithesis of Path #2. If your intention in becoming a writer was to make a name for yourself through achieving literary glory, this is a far cry from that dream. Instead, ghostwriters make a living by doing the hard, thankless work and passing on the credit to someone else.

When I first began ghostwriting political opinion columns for a client, I was angry because my name was unattached. To be perfectly honest, it wounded my ego. I wanted people to know I was the brilliant person behind the article. But I got over it. I realized it was better to be paid nicely to do what I loved than to receive the credit. Besides, many other items I have written have my name attached. I don't need to hog all that glory for myself.

Final note: ghostwriting someone else's book can often be a very intimate experience. Essentially, you're responsible for inhabiting someone else's head and bringing their ideas to life. In my experience, this has meant getting to know some of my clients extremely well. I discuss this reality in further detail in Chapter 10, so I won't spend too much time here on it. You become privy to personal information in this type of collaborative exchange, especially if the ghostwritten assignment is a memoir.

Advantages and Disadvantages of Ghostwriting for Pay:

Advantage: Ghostwriting can be quite lucrative. So-called vanity projects can especially pay well if the client has disposable income.

Advantage: Unlike one-offs, such as blogs, ghostwriting book assignments can be long-term (six months to a year) revenue streams.

Advantage: Ghostwriting is always in demand. There is a huge need for this service, from business owners to celebrities.

Disadvantage: It can be upsetting not to receive public acknowledgement for your hard work. Instead, your client gets the credit.

Disadvantage: Your portfolio can suffer. You can't list ghostwriting assignments on your resume if you are bound to a confidentiality agreement.

Disadvantage: Many ghostwriting book contracts exclude you from further monetization, such as royalties, which go to the "author."

SCREENWRITING

Overview:

Unlike other writing forms (even playwriting), screenwriting is unique because it is generally not enjoyed for its own sake. Unlike a book, which may be considered a finished product, a screenplay is merely a blueprint for an eventual TV show or movie. As such, it is a means to an end.

How does it affect you? The relative production cost of a book is cheap. The publisher simply has to reproduce pages of text. The production costs of making a TV show or movie are much higher. In order to capitalize on your screenwriting, you must convince a decision-maker to see enough value in your words and concept to choose to produce it (in spite of the high costs involved.) Screenwriting can be a highly lucrative form of writing. On the other hand, it can be extremely difficult to break into this field.

What is Expected:

Many people think they can write a movie. They don't understand screenwriting is a specialized craft with its own conventions. If you have never read a screenplay, you should prepare yourself before writing one by reading different examples. Several websites offer famous screenplays you can download for reference.

Beyond the technical aspects, screenwriting has other specific challenges. Unlike some other forms of prose, copious white space is highly desirable. Less is more with screenwriting. No one wants to read a 200-page script with huge text blocks. Use your words sparingly, especially your dialogue. Also, use *Final Draft* or some other accepted software program to screen write. Screenwriting in Microsoft Word is amateurish and will be met with derision by entertainment professionals.

Advantages and Disadvantages of Screenwriting for Pay:

Advantage: Screenwriting can pay extremely well (if it makes it past the gatekeepers and into the hands of the decision-makers.)

Advantage: Screenwriting is very prestigious. If you have success in this field, you can leverage it for more writing assignments.

Advantage: Most laypeople don't know how to format screenplays correctly. If you do, you are in the minority and your professional abilities can command more money.

Disadvantage: Screenplays are notoriously hard to sell. Hollywood is a den of nepotism. Often, it comes down to "who you know," not how good you are.

Disadvantage: There are (monetary) barriers to breaking in. You need to buy expensive software and learn a technical language, which can require years of higher education through film school.

Disadvantage: Unlike books or other forms of prose writing, screenplays don't stand on their own as commodities to be sold but must be produced expensively.

MISCELLANEOUS WRITING

Overview and What is Expected:

Many types of writing fall into this category. Examples include: landing page web copy, manuscript critiques, speechwriting, resume/CV writing, college essay coaching, memos, taglines, brochures. I have taken on all of these assignments at one time or another. Rather than go through all the various items individually, I'll give you an overview. I won't list the advantages and disadvantages, as each project contains its own pluses and minuses.

The three main things you need to project when taking on miscellaneous writing assignment are:

- Professionalism
- Confidence
- Authority

If your goal is to be a *$ix-Figure Writer*, understand the assignments you will get (especially in the beginning) will often be random and piecemeal. It is important for your own personal growth, wallet, and future prospects to attempt them all. Remember the *$ix-Figure Writer Axiom*: "Every interaction with a client (or future client) is a chance to do one of two things: build trust or erode trust."

You want to be known as a reliable writer, someone who can successfully tackle *any* project. The best way to enhance your writing abilities is to step out of your comfort zone and write things that challenge you. These will be beneficial learning experiences for many reasons, but primarily they will teach you what you wish to pursue and what you wish to avoid.

CHAPTER 7 - NETWORKING

"The richest people in the world look for and build networks, everyone else looks for work."

~Robert Kiyosaki

As previously discussed, the common perception of the writer is a loner: the man or woman who sits at the computer typing away, slaving over words. This stereotype may represent you. Perhaps you're an introvert who likes to work alone in your apartment. Fine. Creating content can be a solitary affair. But when it comes to monetizing, you need to come out of your shell. Get over your shyness. Temporarily become an extrovert. Unless you're the literary genius exception who can compel publishers, editors, and agents to bang down your door, you need social connections to grow your business.

The Case for Collaboration

In spite of the lone writer stereotype, many top-earning writers are collaborators who enjoy working with one or more partners. Why is this ideal? Just take the book you are reading. It was written collaboratively. The old cliché "two heads are better than one" applies. Sham and I come from diverse backgrounds and have different skillsets. This diversity allowed us the opportunity to bounce ideas off one another for instant feedback. You will gain this benefit as well when working with someone else.

Time Management

As a writer, your time is money. And nothing is more time-consuming (and therefore expensive) then wasting it by making bad creative decisions. You can avoid this pitfall through collaboration. Before typing a word of our eventual manuscript, Sham and I discussed every aspect during a thorough outlining process. We weeded out the bad ideas and improved the good ones to determine what to include, saving us gobs of time. This is the template for an ideal writing partnership across all categories, fiction and nonfiction.

Dispense with Your Ego. Your Bank Account Will Thank You

If your ego requires that *your* name be listed on *your* book in big letters, good luck. Perhaps it will happen for you. But why not play it smart? If you are willing to check your ego at the door, you may discover having a good partner will allow you to be immensely more productive. Just think of all the projects you could complete faster with another person working alongside you, sharing the workload.

But If I Work Alone, Won't I Earn More Money?

Sometimes. But not necessarily. Let me give you an example. Some time ago, I was hired to write an adaptation screenplay. Not only did the project pay well, but also the person who commissioned me is well known and has a great social network of potential future clients.

The problem I found was, while her book was an interesting memoir, it did not readily lend itself to cinematic adaptation. For several days, I wallowed in a funk. (If you recall the movie, *Adaptation,* then you will have an idea of the deep havoc a challenging creative project can wreak on the psyche.) I simply could not find a way into the story to make the main character sympathetic and/or interesting to watch onscreen.

The more I fretted over screwing up the assignment, the more I worried about the social blowback. The individual who hired me had made a big point of telling her contacts how excited she was to work with me. I feared what she would tell the same people if I botched her project. Goodbye, future projects.

Then I wised up. I called Charles, my old screenwriting partner, and offered to pay him a portion of the commission to help me outline the project. Sure, it set me back a few dollars in the short term. I could have pocketed it if I went it alone. But in the end, it *saved* me money. Working with my buddy, who is terrific when it comes to story, allowed me to find the human angle.

Within a weekend (working twelve to fourteen hours a day), we knocked out a killer outline. It became the blueprint for an excellent screenplay. Yes, I did have to part with some of the money I might have kept for myself, but without Charles's invaluable insight, I doubt I could have cracked the story.

Working collaboratively saved me hours, *if not days,* of potentially wasted time. Most importantly, I adhered to the *$ix-Figure Writer Axiom.* By pleasing the client, I earned her trust and grew my social network. When the project was finished, she happily recommended me to more friends who wanted my services, thereby increasing my income. If I had been shortsighted about losing a little money or prideful about asking for help, my business would have suffered.

The Need for Networking: No One is an Island

Networking is the natural culmination of all the concepts we have previously discussed. Whether or not your content creation occurs in a vacuum, the marketing and promotion of your services cannot. You need to meet people to get work.

Please note: when I speak of social networking, I don't mean the digital kind. I am talking about old-fashioned, press-the-flesh encounters. Digital social networking can be a great model for many types of businesses, but not the *$ix-Figure Writer*. Though *$ix-Figure Writers* must use web platforms for distribution and audience building, they grow their client base through face-to-face interactions, which engender trust and accord.

$ix-Figure Writer Tip: Don't rely on email or phone calls to make sales connections. Set yourself apart from other business folks afraid to meet face-to-face and establish personal connections with potential clients.

Some writers (especially pre-Internet) were highly successful without networking. These lucky ones were able to get lucrative assignments or book deals without venturing into the social sphere. Good for them. It has not been my experience, and I doubt it will be yours either. The single most helpful thing I did to grow my writing business is to meet people face-to-face.

If you have ever been in sales, think about networking as a numbers game. Similar to dating, the wider you spread your social net, the more opportunities you have to interact. The more interactions you have, the more opportunities you have to sell. The more sales attempts, the more likely you are to convert.

You can call yourself a writer. You can make business cards, which proclaim you are a writer. But if you are not earning a living from as one, it does you no good. *Other* people need to know of you as a writer. They need to meet you in person. They need to shake your hand. Most of all, they need to know how your profession can help them. Consequently, you need to put yourself in as many different possible social situations as you can think of. What do I mean by that?

Join the Chamber of Commerce? But I'm a Writer

By all means, join your city's Chamber of Commerce. These organizations are strategic hubs for stimulating businesses networking opportunities. My prediction? You will be the only person representing your industry. Good. Less competition for you.

When I first joined my city's Chamber of Commerce, I was blown away by the positive reception. No writer had ever joined the Chamber before. If you've ever been involved in these kinds of small business networks, you will undoubtedly observe the same kinds of industries appear without fail: insurance, mortgage lending, estate planning, plumbing, accounting, etc. Just try to imagine for a second how *boring* it is for the Chamber members to hear the same spiel again and again.

Enter the writer. Suddenly, the group has something novel to discuss. No pun intended. People gravitate toward writers. Small business owners will be curious about you because you don't fit into the mold. Cash in on that intrigue by pitching your services. As mentioned, every business needs a writer. Here is a list of some writing categories you can sell: social media, ghostwriting, web copy, copywriting, journalism, miscellaneous writing, even screenwriting or vanity book projects.

Find a way to connect with business owners, and you will have opportunities to grow your writing business. Beyond your city's Chamber of Commerce, here are ten other organizations to consider joining:

- Business Networking International (BNI Groups)
- LeTip International
- The Rotary Club
- Chambers of Commerce in *other* nearby cities (you often don't have to live in a city to be a member of its Chamber)
- Women's Groups
- Religious Organizations
- Mastermind Groups
- The Convention and Visitor's Bureau
- The Kiwanis Club
- The Optimists Club

Bonus organization to try: Toastmasters United. Not only does it offer a great way to practice your speaking/pitching skills, it gives you a captive forum to educate others about your business.

EXERCISE: Make a Good First Impression on Other Business Owners at Your First Networking Event

STEP ONE: Rehearse both a ten- and a thirty-second infomercial you can deliver to explain your business. The former is for meeting individuals one-on-one. The latter is for pitching your services in a group setting.

STEP TWO: Bring lots of business cards with you. Try to give one out to each person you meet and take theirs. The day after an event, send each person you met a thoughtful email, thanking them for speaking with you. Make sure to write something about setting up a future one-on-one meeting to learn about their business needs.

STEP THREE: Try to meet everyone you can but don't be afraid to spend extra time with those people who express special interest in your services. It's better to go deep, than to go wide. Building a solid rapport with just one person can be far more advantageous than superficially chatting with many different lukewarm prospects.

CAUTION: Many business-networking events involve alcohol. If you decide to partake, limit yourself to two drinks maximum. It is okay to be social, but don't overdo it. Not only do you want a clear head for remembering all the people you meet, your purpose is to impress others with your professionalism. Getting tipsy, not to mention drunk, is a sure-fire way to shoot yourself in the foot.

Go to Writers Conferences

But aren't writing conferences just for improving your craft? And don't they cost a lot of money? Yes, writing conferences can help you become a better writer. And yes, they will set you back monetarily. But let's discuss why they help with social networking if you follow Path #2.

To the first point, writing conferences generally involve keynote industry speakers as well as smaller breakout sessions for perfecting your craft. I have attended several such conferences for SCBWI, the Society of Children's Book Writers and Illustrators. Beyond the valuable education I received, I had an opportunity to hobnob with decisions-makers I ordinarily wouldn't be exposed to. This is the value for the high entry cost.

Writing conferences can be expensive. But the hefty price tag serves the same purpose as the cost to join some business organizations. The high price of both helps vet the professional from the unprofessional. In some sense, it strategically turns away all but the most serious-minded. Those who are left are invested monetarily. They are presumably willing to make important sacrifices because they value what these social interactions will bring.

The editors and agents who attend conferences know this. It's why they are more willing to accept unsolicited manuscripts from participants. By installing a paywall, the decisions-makers are hedging their bets with confidence the material they will receive is of higher, more professional quality. (Then again, it can also come from untalented amateurs who don't mind shelling out dough. You never know.)

Theoretically, the money involved and the instructive aspect of conferences go hand-in-hand. The organizations, which put on writing conferences, need to have an ostensible purpose for meeting. Therefore, they provide valuable information. The same logic applies to Chamber of Commerce mixers. Nearly every event involves an educational aspect. For instance, business owners are given the opportunity to educate members about their businesses. Underlying each event is the true, unspoken purpose: the opportunity to meet other professionals in your field as potential clients. (And for writing conferences: the influential decision-makers.)

Bringing It All Together

If you recall, I suggested the best route for being successful as a *$ix-Figure Writer* is to both sell your writing *and* your services. Participating in a networking group, like your city's Chamber of Commerce, is the ideal way to make money through selling your services (Path #1). Attending Writers Conferences is a strategic way to sell your writing by meeting decision-makers who may become interested in your work. (Path #2).

Chapter 9 will help you market yourself. For now, the important takeaway from this chapter is in order to be successful with either Path, (not to mention Path #3) you need to make personal, face-to-face connections.

Chapter Summary

- In spite of the stereotypical perception of a successful writer as one who works alone, it is far better to work collaboratively.
- Working collaboratively can be helpful for the *$ix-Figure Writer* because it saves valuable time. Two heads (or more) are usually better than one. Bouncing ideas off another and getting immediate feedback are two such examples.
- Get over your need to hog the credit and/or money on writing projects. Another reason to work with other writers is, by sharing the workload, you can be more productive.
- Face-to-face networking is essential to growing your business as a *$ix-Figure Writer* (following Path #1). One of the best ways to connect to small business owners is through joining local networking groups, such as your city's Chamber of Commerce.
- Attending Writers Conferences is an excellent way to make personal connections to decision-makers and sell your own writing (Path #2). Similar to

business networking groups, the time and money you spend at these functions can pay off handsomely through deep personal connections.

Action Steps:

- Find other writers to collaborate on projects. One good way to find them is by using your critique group to determine who is a possible personality match.
- Drop your ego. Don't be resistant to pair up with other writers. In the long run, it will save you time and money. Additionally, the creative output will be strengthened through the increased brainpower.
- Join the Chamber of Commerce and other local networking groups. Get your name and face out there.
- Don't be afraid to volunteer on committees of local groups. You'll find the more you give to others, the more they want to help you with your business.
- Attend Writers Conferences to meet decision-makers who may decide to publish your work.

CHAPTER 8 - WRITING AS A CAREER

"Amateurs sit and wait for inspiration, the rest of us just get up and go to work."

~Stephen King

One day, I sat in traffic evaluating my life and was struck by an incredible thought: *I am a writer.* All my family's income comes from stories or ideas I think up and words I write on a computer. Pretty cool, huh? Even cooler was this experience. I was sitting on the bed with my wife itemizing the money I had made that calendar year, and it occurred to me: I had made six figures as a writer!

These types of experiences could be yours too.

Writing as a Political Statement

Michael

I always hated authority. In elementary and middle school, my teachers sent me to the principal's office all the time. This disdain for the powers that be didn't end when I joined the workforce. If anything, it multiplied. I despised taking orders. It pissed me off that no matter how well I performed my duties, I could still be fired for no cause at any time. I even developed anxiety about losing my job. It wasn't based on anything I had done. It was based on the unfairness of my situation. I had no leverage. My livelihood was dependent on the actions of my employer.

Once I made enough money from writing to drop out permanently, a weight lifted. I realized I never had to go back to being someone's employee. Want to know what that feels like? *Freedom.*

It infected my whole being with lightness and joy. I used to dread Sunday nights because I knew the next day I would be someone's wage slave. Now I love them. Do you know why? For one thing, I get to do what I love. For another, I design my day. I pick what assignments I take. I choose which customers to work with. I have autonomy. And all the money I make goes to my family, not my boss.

This can be your life, too.

Let's go over some fundamentals to consider when turning writing into a six-figure career.

Your Portfolio: Trade on What You Have

As a writer, you live and die based on your portfolio. At least you do in the beginning when you're starting out. People want to know what you have done so they know whether to trust you. (Again, remember the *$ix-Figure Writer Axiom*.) It's a reasonable concern. After all, unlike other vocations, such as plumbing, writing is subjective. Because of writing's perception-based nature, these three things can produce or destroy trust for any writer:

- Your Persona
- Your Work
- What Past Clients Say About Your Work

We have already gone into #1 and #3 in detail, so I won't discuss them here. Let's talk about #2, your work. Your portfolio demonstrates what you have done. These days, it's rare to see someone carting around a physical portfolio. Instead, writers place their work online where people can access it. Your personal web page is a good place. I show my work on *Pinterest* because it presents the content in a beautiful, user-friendly way.

This section is meant only to emphasize the importance of having a portfolio. If you are a working writer, you already know this. The important idea is to leverage your successes. Every time you complete an assignment, add the work to your ongoing portfolio. Then ask for a testimonial for your website. If the clients are happy with your work, they will do so gladly. (If your client is unhappy with your work, walk away. Hopefully, you were paid and learned something.)

What you are building through your portfolio is more than just entries. You are creating a *reputation* you can trade upon. In the new Connection Economy, one of your primary assets is how people think of you. The more people who can vouch for the great work you've done, the better your opportunity for future success.

In addition, the more prestigious the work you do, the better you will be thought of, and the more you will be paid. During every business-networking group, I am supposed to get up and talk about myself. When I do, I tailor the conversation to the room.

If I'm trying to get social media clients, I mention how I wrote web copy and managed social media for a celebrity's charity. If I am trying to get ghostwriting clients, it's trickier. Legally, I am barred from mentioning clients' names. Instead, I say I have worked with philanthropists and individuals related to the entertainment industry. When it comes to screenwriting, I can point to having read scripts professionally for the president of CAA. I can mention selling a movie treatment to Disney.

Think of people you have worked with and refer to them each time you are asked for your portfolio and what have you done.

Working Free: Yes, I Advocate This

Some logical concerns about the last section might be: "But what if my portfolio is lacking? What if I don't have anything worth including? What if I haven't been paid yet as a writer?"

First, never say those things to any client. Keep the information to yourself. Just like no one wants to be the first person a surgeon practices on, no one wants to be your first client. Here is how to handle this dilemma: offer to do free work.

Start with friends and family. Let's say your father-in-law owns a contracting business. Ask him to let you write a free blog on his website. The next time a potential client wants to see your work, show them the terrific blog you wrote on contracting. Don't mention you did it free or that the person you wrote it for is your father-in-law. The potential client doesn't need to know how much you were paid or the person's relation to you. It's none of their business. All that matters is the fine work you did.

Take this idea and run with it. Do as many freebie assignments as you need until you have a competitive portfolio. Then stop. If you've been successful, perhaps some of the people you've given free work will hire you because they like the content you've written for them. This is an excellent way to grow your business.

EXERCISE: Two More Suggestions to Break Into Writing When You Have No Clients

Try any of the following to jump-start your writing career.

SUGGESTION ONE: Target a niche. Go after one type of business and then pitch your services to clientele within that category. For instance, let's say you have an interest in wellness and know a lot about the subject. Approach all the local practitioners in your area. Pitch yourself as an expert who will help their potential customers understand the need for their business through your copywriting services.

SUGGESTION TWO: Create your own blog in which you selflessly promote others. Everyone loves to get praise and recognition for their work. Establish a blog in which you spotlight individuals you would like to write for. Say positive things about them on your blog, and then establish some traffic by promoting the blog via Twitter and through your personal social media connections, such as friends and family. At the very least, the individual will be flattered. Then again, they might hire you to write more things about them if they like the increased attention.

Setting Your Rates

There are many different ways to structure payment when you sell your writing services.

A Word of Caution:

This applies to each category. Be sure to charge enough. Don't undervalue your services, especially when you are starting out. People will take advantage of you. They will label you as cheap. When you finally charge what you should have charged in the first place, they will complain about paying you more. I learned this lesson the hard way.

Pricing by the Hour

Sometimes I am asked to do this, especially when the job is on a consulting basis. It's a straightforward way of billing. It's the optimal way to charge clients when you are doing social media outreach, typically responding to posts and/or messages in real-time.

Pricing by the Word

This can be an effective way to bill when you are working on blogs, web copy, journalistic articles, and ghostwriting books. It's ideal because there is no haggling with the client over the time you spend working. The final word count is self-evident.

You need to determine a rate that works for you and the client's budget. I have seen professional writers who charge $1 per word and others who charge much less. Negotiate the sweet spot between what the client can reasonably afford and what you expect.

Pricing by the Project

I recommend this for screenwriting projects especially. The reason is you don't know how much time it will take to write the outline and then the script. (It's possible to estimate of course, but you have no way of truly knowing.)

What you can point to with the client are *milestones* or benchmarks for deliverables. I frequently use this language in my contracts for screenwriting: "There is a retainer to begin the project, i.e. do the brainstorming/outlining process. The next deliverable will be considered the first act of the screenplay, and the final two acts will be considered the final deliverables for purposes of billing."

Get Everything in Writing

If a person wants to work with you but won't sign a contract, don't agree. Politely walk away. It comes down to trust. Trust goes both ways. If you cannot trust someone to put an agreement in writing, you probably cannot trust the person to pay you.

In general, every project you undertake needs to have an explicit contract, which lists both parties' responsibilities. It should also list due dates for deliverables, remuneration amounts, and who owns the work.

> **$ix-Figure Writer Tip:** Never agree to work with someone on spec in lieu of paying you. Avoid the person who says, "I can't pay you now, but this project will make you tons of money."

One note about the above tip: this situation never ends well. The only time to write on spec is when you conceive of the project and are willing to take the personal risk. Do not believe those individuals who refuse to pay you with promises of future returns. They will never pay you, nor will you make tons of money from their project. I know this from personal experience.

Revisions

Always include a reasonable fee for edits. Don't make the same mistake I did when starting out as a *$ix-Figure Writer*. I didn't allot fees for these time-consuming activities. Always remember, writing is a highly subjective vocation. You may think you are finished, but the client may not.

Be willing to make reasonable alterations to your content in a timely manner. If you do so, you will satisfy the *$ix-Figure Writer Axiom*. By earning trust and goodwill, you will continue to earn future assignments as well as referrals.

However, problems can ensue if you find yourself working with a client who makes unreasonable demands on your time. These difficult individuals can be under the delusion you will continue working forever on their project. This is why it is so important to include special language in all your contracts: "Revisions will be billed to the client." A good rule of thumb is to charge a little more than half your hourly price for these modifications. If you do so, you will find even formerly "perfectionist" clients tend to let go when they know they will be billed for additional changes.

But some of them don't. Here are some examples of clients you may encounter.

Types of Clients You May Encounter

The following are generalizations of potential client personality traits. They are by no means comprehensive. Human beings differ widely, and clients may exhibit these traits in varying degrees. The intention is to prepare you for your potential clients.

The Easy-Peasy Client

The dream come true client. This gracious person makes few demands on your time and trusts your vision when it comes to generating their content. They pay on time (or upfront), and when the project is over, they applaud your work and recommend you to others.

Actively seek out these individuals. They *are* out there, God love 'em.

The High-Strung White-Knuckler

Every time you speak to these clients, your heart speeds up. Your stomach tightens. They don't respond to emails in a timely manner. They miss meetings, and their demands are unrealistic. They want everything done yesterday and don't understand what can be accomplished.

If you can avoid working with them, steer clear. They are bound to cause problems and suck up your time. If they pay well and you find yourself contracting with them, get everything in writing upfront.

The Detail-Oriented Backseat Writer

Though these people hire you to write their copy or ghostwrite their books, sometimes you wonder why since they rewrite everything you produce. Each time you turn in a deliverable, they send you long emails with notes about things you need to change. Though they hire you, it quickly becomes clear they want to redo everything. These people are highly critical of your creative work.

It's best to avoid contracting with these individuals if you can identify them early. If not, remember to speak up for your vision (if you think you are right), but always remember you are in a client-to-client relationship. They are not your bosses. If you feel your talents are being dismissed or you are not receiving the money such handholding demands, extricate yourself from the situation.

The Emotionally Uninvolved Professional

This is a slight variation on the Easy-Peasy Client and is a godsend in a different way. Though they may not fawn over your work and gush about the great material you are putting out, it's fine because you can enjoy their detached professionalism. They respond to email, phone calls, and texts promptly while giving you unambiguous instructions. They may not necessarily brag to their friends about your work because it's not their personality type, but their sheer professionalism makes working with them a joy.

Actively seek out these individuals.

The Overpromiser/Overtalker/Un-follow-througher

This is an umbrella designation for anyone who promises things and doesn't deliver. Sometimes these are pseudo-clients. You meet with them, and they say you are hired and they can't wait to work together.

Then they never call you again and ignore your emails. These are also the individuals who suggest you work on spec because they have "connections" and if you do this with them, you will strike it rich. Last, they are the types of clients who tell you they plan to do many things but never ever follow through on them.

Unfortunately, individuals with the above traits tend to be common, especially when you are starting your business. Stay away from these people. Even if they promise big money, don't get involved without a signed contract. In the long run, you will save yourself time and needless suffering. Last, if you are uncertain whether you may be dealing with this kind of client, set a trial period and see how they perform. If they flake out more than once, disengage.

Bidding on Work

I rarely bid on projects. However, sometimes clients will ask several writers to try out for jobs in the same way actors audition, or perhaps more aptly, as contractors are asked to bid on construction projects.

I have found that this is usually a bad deal as it reduces your leverage. When you are up against others for the same job, someone may underprice you. Why put yourself in the position of cutting your rates to obtain a project? If clients measure you against someone else based on price (as opposed to quality), they probably don't value your expertise and are looking for low rates.

Usually, someone can underbid you. Move on. (I recently heard about some bloggers who charge five dollars per hour for their services. How can you expect to compete with them if your goal is to earn a living?) Retreat. Live to fight another day. More opportunities will be available to receive better pay for your work.

Chapter Summary

- One major benefit of being a *$ix-Figure Writer* is the freedom it affords you to be self-employed. Opting out of the wage slave game frees you from the vulnerability that comes from having a boss who can fire you at whim.

- Building a solid portfolio is one of the best ways to demonstrate your worth to clients.

- Leverage each past success in your portfolio and build a reputation based on the clients who have commissioned you.

- Working without payment is a good idea when starting out. Every *$ix-Figure Writer* has to begin somewhere. You can parlay this experience into improving your portfolio to earn future writing assignments.

- There are many ways to determine your rates: pricing by the hour, pricing by the word, and pricing by the project are several.

- When billing, it is important to remember to charge for any edits and not undervalue yourself.

- All contracts must be in writing and explicitly list each party's responsibilities.

- Identify which clients to avoid and gravitate towards. Be mindful of who you are dealing with to make the correct choice.

- Avoid bidding against others because someone else can always undercut you based on price, not quality.

Action Steps:

- Drop out of the corporate workforce as a W-2 employee. As soon as you can, begin working for yourself.
- Create a solid portfolio based on clients you have worked with.
- Ask each client to be included in your ongoing portfolio to establish a winning reputation.
- Don't feel bad about working free in the beginning while you are starting out.
- Determine the best way to bill for each project based on what is required.
- Ensure all your writing assignments have a written contract.
- Avoid time-sucking, difficult clients. Gravitate towards clients from whom you will earn the most money and be pleasant to work with.
- Avoid bidding against your competition. Instead, go after those clients who value quality, not the cheapest price.

CHAPTER 9 - MARKETING YOURSELF

"If people like you they will listen to you, but if they trust you, they will do business with you."

~Zig Ziglar

"The most important thing to remember is to know your audience."

~Lewis Howes

The idea of someone making a six-figure income through writing is such an anomaly non-believers will constantly doubt you. This chapter is about steering business conversations from the fantastical to the practical when selling your services or your creative writing. Convert future clients into actual clients by employing each tool at your disposal: professionalism, ability, experience, expertise, and even personal charm. If you are successful in marketing yourself, you may be as amazed as non-believers to learn it is possible to earn a living doing what you love.

Pitching

Michael

I once took a class on pitching. The professor who taught it believed in long-form pitches, and our final exam involved getting in front of a room of our peers to tell the whole story in a ten-minute, uninterrupted block. Why is this a terrible idea?

First, when pitching in the real world, you will never have this much time. No one will sit around, listening to you talk for that long. Everyone is busy, especially professionals and business owners. Believing they would allow you to drone on and on is absurd.

What's far more important than memorizing a lengthy explanation of your project or services is coming up with a thirty-second "elevator pitch." The idea behind this concept is you should be able to get through the important, *sellable* aspects of your idea in the time it takes to a ride in an elevator with a decision-maker to your respective floors.

Keep it Simple, Keep It Focused

We've all had the annoying experience of listening to someone blather on about themselves. Don't be that person. Instead, laser-focus on what you think your audience cares about. Then spend all your time speaking to it. Let me give you an example. I recently attended a BNI meeting where I was asked to deliver a thirty-second commercial for my company.

Here is how I broke down my commercial pitch:

1-5 seconds:

I gave my company name. I explained I am a writer who owns a writing services company specializing in creative content. I cited my MFA in screenwriting from Chapman University.

Why? Credibility. Not only did I go to school for writing, I have a related graduate degree from a top school. Next, I used buzzwords like creative content, to make my listeners understand I'm not talking about antiquated copywriting but web copy and new forms of media. In addition, I mentioned my company. This indicates prestige, not freelance amateurishness.

5-20 seconds:

I discussed the major projects I have worked on: selling a treatment to Disney, which was made into a movie, being commissioned to write a novel at a major publisher, being hired to ghostwrite books and columns for celebrities.

Why? Experience and success matter. Major projects indicate levels of professionalism commensurate with higher pay and status. If any audience members were ready to write me off based on my unusual vocation, they surely took note and listened. Instead of wondering how a writer who isn't Dean Koontz, makes a living, their thoughts might have switched to, "Might I have a need for a writer? This guy's the real deal." Good. I've given them the value proposition.

20-30 seconds:

Wrap-up. I explained the writing services my company provides while being mindful of the room. For instance, I might have said I offer social media content, such as blogs, or I ghostwrite business books if I thought a potentially interested client attended. I told my audience what I could offer them, turning the conversation toward how I could be of service.

Why? Always tailor your message to the people who may pay for your product or services. Don't waste people's time (and your own) by going into something in which they aren't interested. Try to anticipate people's needs so you can satisfy them, thereby earning their business. Last, close with a call to action, such as, "My business is here to meet all your writing needs."

Always Keep It Interesting

This advice applies to both pitching your writing services and selling your own writing. Much as the *$ix-Figure Writer Axiom* encourages you to view every encounter as an opportunity to build trust, you must also view each pitch as a chance to build interest in your work. Get people fired up about working with you and/or your project(s).

When it comes to selling your own creative writing, here are three ways to build interest:

Logline:

This harkens back to the need for simplicity. You want people to understand what your project is in one pithy, enticing sentence. Here's an absurd example: "My comedic novel is about a male stripper who invents a time machine to go back in time to sponge off hot, wealthy sugar mommies throughout recorded history. The working title is *Time Traveler Gigolo*."

Build Stakes:

Why should decision-makers care? Within your brief pitch, quickly establish an emotional connection. Stakes provide gravitas, a reason for your listener to become invested emotionally. For instance, if you were pitching *Hunger Games* for the first time as your own material, you'd want to emphasize young people are forced to fight to the death to save their families. Also, Katniss, our heroine, is willing to lay down her own life for the little sister she loves.

Give Them Novelty:

Aristotle once said there are only two kinds of stories: love and tragedy. Joseph Campbell simplified this even further by suggesting there is but one plot: the so-called "Monomyth." While there may be a finite number of story categories, everything under the sun has *not* already been written. Not by a long shot. The world craves novelty. Your job as a creative person is to give your audience something interesting and surprising. Emphasis on surprising. Shock us. Titillate us. But please don't bore us.

EXERCISE: Practice Writing Your Own Logline

A Logline distills your story elements into a succinct one-to-two sentence description. Try this step-by-step guide to craft yours.

STEP ONE: Identify the protagonist, the antagonist, and the protagonist's goal.

STEP TWO: Identify why the protagonist cannot reach the goal.

STEP THREE: Find an adjective to describe the protagonist but avoiding use a proper name (like Chuck) to describe the character.

STEP FOUR: Include stakes and a setup for your protagonist. Create a viable world or backdrop for your story.

STEP FIVE: Don't reveal the ending. You want to sell the sizzle, not the steak. Entice your audience. Make them want to know more.

Querying: The Ninth Circle of Hell

This advice relates to selling your creative work. Many informative books and articles have been written on this subject, so I won't bore you with the technical details. Instead, I will offer some philosophical points from my own experience. Also, if you are interested in knowing more about the subject of querying from experts, check the following websites:

www.AgentQuery.com

This covers basics, such as which agents/editors to approach, what these folks prefer, and how to reach them. (As well as many other helpful items.)

www.QueryTracker.com

Similar to *Agent Query*, this great resource is constantly updated to provide you with crucial information to pitch to the right person in the right way. A word of caution: always double-check the website of the professional you intend to pitch to make sure the information is up-to-date and accurate.

www.WritersDigest.com

Another helpful resource actually provides real-world examples of query letters from writers to agents, which worked. A valuable read, this site discusses pertinent query considerations, such as the appropriate length and what to include in your letter.

My Personal Thoughts on Querying

Querying is a gruesome, thankless business, which can eat hours of your time and swallow up huge reserves of your self-esteem. The ugly truth is agents/editors get hundreds of unsolicited query letters every day. Can you imagine what it is like for these professionals to sift through so much content?

Agents work solely on commission. They don't receive payment unless they pick winners who will make them money. Since the vast majority of writing is mediocre at best, and tear-your-eyes-out-god-awful at worst, agents must be extremely discerning with their time. They know the odds of finding the jewel among so much garbage is low. Consequently, they put most of their energy into receiving material through more reliable means, such as vetted referrals.

Does this mean a debut writer needs to have an agent *to land an agent?* Pretty much. It's a gut-wrenching *Catch 22:* you need an agent to get a book published, but you also need to have a book published to get an agent. (By the way, the same logic applies with getting an agent for film or TV.)

What to Do?

Here are my suggestions:

Engage. But Remember It's a Numbers Game

You need to write query letters. In my lifetime, I have created over a thousand iterations for various projects. A well-crafted query can help your chances of getting published and/or representation, so gaining proficiency in this form of writing will be helpful. It allows you to think in commercial terms.

By paring down your writing to bare, sellable essentials, you learn to pitch your project and yourself. No agent may ever favorably respond to your query letters, but through the process of distilling your ideas, your pitching skills will improve. When placed in a room with decision-makers, you'll know the right things to say to sell your project.

Next, don't be too discouraged about the lack of progress when it comes to querying. We have all heard the statistics about successful books that were turned down initially. *Chicken Soup for the Soul* received a whopping 140 rejection letters. Keep trying. If your work is good, you are bound to get it into the right person's hands eventually.

Make Personal Connections Not Just Cyber Connections

If you go to www.WritersDigest.com, all the writers whose work was bought based on their email queries may hearten you. It may inspire you to believe such possibilities exist for you as a writer.

Your query letter (one of hundreds received daily) could reach the right person and strike them with just the right impression to offer you your dream, but the reality is those outcomes are rare. (They *are* still possible, though.) You increase your chances of conversion substantially by establishing a personal connection with a decision-maker. This is why I highly recommend Writers Conferences where you have the chance to meet agents and editors in the flesh.

A personal connection to a decision-maker elevates your status. It sets you apart from the sea of unknown hordes beating down the cyber door with demanding queries. The success I had in getting requests for a full manuscript read came from such a personal connection, not a cold email. I was introduced to the keynote speaker/agent at a SCBWI conference. He requested I send him my first two chapters. I also met another editor at the bar between breakout sessions. I quickly pitched him my book (It took less than twenty seconds). He found the idea interesting and asked me to send him the full manuscript.

Pick Yourself

This was covered in Chapter 5, but it bears repeating. By all means, try to get paid or published the traditional way, but don't stop there, and don't allow yourself to be defined by what others think of you. Uber-marketing genius, Seth Godin, planted the seed for this idea with his prescient book, *The Icarus Deception*. I recommend you read it. The easiest way to become a *$ix-Figure Writer* is to discard the idea the only way to succeed is to wait for someone else to pick you.

The fact is, no one may pick you. Therefore, you must pick yourself.

If no one's publishing you, publish yourself. Build your own platform to bypass the traditional system. You may fail, but at least it will be based on your own efforts and abilities, not because someone else didn't value you.

Contests

The screenwriting world is filled with high-exposure competitions, such as *Blue Cat, The Nicholl, Blacklist* and *Scriptapalooza,* to name a few. In addition, other similar opportunities to receive the notice of decision-makers exist, such as *Virtual PitchFest.* Explore these ventures. Apply to writing fellowships, such as those offered by Fox, Disney, and Warner Brothers. Some of them even offer stipends. The outcome of being selected or even nominated for any of the above will be extremely positive. It will fast track your writing career, earning you the notice of agents and other individuals who can help you.

Many contests for all kinds of other writing are available, including manuscripts, short stories, essays, and poems. I mention the screenwriting contests because I have had personal experience with them. I have not applied to many of the other kinds of writing contests, but I understand their value. Like the screenplay competitions, they give you a chance to shine among so many other creatives in your field.

Here are some good literary contests to help you get an edge on Path #2, Selling your Writing:

The Writer's Digest Annual Writing Competition

National Book Foundation

The Pinch Literary Awards

The William Van Dyke Short Story Contest

Centre for Literature Publishing-Nelligan Prize

A Word of Caution:

Contests can be expensive. In one year, I spent close to $1,500 in competition fees. How much good did it do me? I got the notice of some professionals after placing in several contests and winning one. The downside is the considerable expense. It's a gamble. If you do not place or win anything, you stand to lose a lot of your hard-earned cash. This may not bother you. But then, there are many other free ways to become noticed.

Maintain a Strong Online Presence

You should know this already. If you don't exist online, you don't exist to many people. I am not suggesting you create a Facebook page to post enticing pictures of your meals. And I definitely discourage you from letting your zany friends tag you in compromising photos. This is the opposite of a recipe for success.

Remember the *$ix-Figure Writer Axiom* when it comes to maintaining your social media platforms. Each website, from Facebook to Twitter, should be an opportunity to project professionalism to build trust and rapport with the web community. Put your best foot forward in every digital space. You never know who may be searching you.

Live By This Motto: Give and You Shall Receive

Don't be the person who brags about your successes online. It's not just tacky, it's bad business. No one is drawn to the people who won't stop yapping about themselves at the party. When engaging socially online, build others up. Not yourself.

***$ix-Figure Writer* Tip:** Avoid promoting yourself online. Instead, spend your time promoting others, and you will be rewarded.

Here's an example: Instead of tweeting about your own upcoming cyberpunk anthology to build your brand momentum, turn the conversation toward promoting other authors in your genre. Get the word out about your peers. Tell the world all the good things they are doing. If you build up other people, especially other writers, you will achieve surprisingly positive results. It may sound trite and sappy, but the more you give online, the more you shall receive.

Don't Let Friends Wreck Your Rep

Purge your social media platforms of troublemakers. Don't give your fun-loving friends a chance to write something ignorant on your wall. Think about it. You've spent so much time establishing a solid image. Why risk all that goodwill by allowing knuckleheads the opportunity to make you look bad?

You can be friends with these kinds of people in real life if you choose. No one's stopping you. But if your goal is to convey professionalism to clients and potential clients, you need to jettison the walking landmines from blowing up your reputation. The last thing you want to do is damage control. It's hugely time-consuming and embarrassing. I know from personal experience. Last, if you're on LinkedIn, make sure you have 500+ connections. You just look better.

Never, Never Complain

A final word about marketing yourself. There is no room for complaining. Pessimism and poor attitude do you no favors. To reference her wonderful book, *Big Magic* once again, Elizabeth Gilbert discusses the amazing gratitude she feels about living a life of writing. Gilbert goes so far as to suggest she would not only willingly eat her own "shit sandwich" of defeat; she would eat anyone else's too. This is how much she loves what she does. You need to project her kind of resilience if you wish to be a *$ix-Figure Writer* for the long haul.

Drop your qualms about what you are not getting. Not only do they bum out the rest of us, *they hurt you*. Do you really think anyone wants to work with someone who denigrates his or her own occupation? Sure, writing can be hard. But so can anything. Complaining about it won't help. It will only diminish you in the eyes of all those people who need to perceive you as confident, talented, and easy to work with.

Undoubtedly, you will have moments of anguish, sadness, anger, frustration, and even despair in your career. It is far better to work through these moments with a positive, grateful attitude. Use your setbacks to fine-tune your approach. Gain wisdom from your losses to discover what you can do better next time. And if you must cry on someone's shoulder, do it privately with your trusted confidantes away from the rest of us who are trying to earn a six-figure living.

You may think I am harsh, but I will explain my rationale. I have worked for fifteen years as a professional writer. I have been cheated out of money and had ideas stolen from me. I've often worked without pay with no hope of money in sight. Yet, if I had to live this life over again, I wouldn't change it. I love what I do. Writing has brought me so much joy. Consequently, I'd never be so disrespectful as to impugn my craft with cynicism and complaints. Besides, what good would it do?

Chapter Summary

- One of the best strategies to marketing yourself as a *$ix-Figure Writer* is to perfect your pitch.
- The most successful pitches are short, simple, and focused.

- When marketing either your writing services or your own writing, generate interest from your audience.
- Three key items to develop interest when selling a story include: a strong logline, dramatic stakes, and surprising novelty.
- Querying can be an effective way to market yourself, but the chances of success are small. Combine querying with personal connections to improve your chances.
- Practice querying because it builds helpful pitching skills, but don't become too discouraged if you don't receive positive results. By picking yourself, you retain the power in your writing career.
- Writing contests can be a good way to attract the attention of decision-makers when marketing your creative writing, but the application fees can be expensive.
- Maintaining a strong online presence is a must for any *$ix-Figure Writer*.
- Complaining is not recommended.

Action Steps:

- Practice your pitching skills often in varying settings when selling your services or your writing. Develop a solid ten-second version and a thirty-second version.

- When selling your writing, focus on crafting a logline to distill your concept down to one powerful sentence.
- Always remember your audience. When pitching your services, try to anticipate a potential client's business needs. When pitching your writing, focus on building interest through a concise but compelling logline, dramatic stakes, and novelty.
- Send out query letters to market your creative writing and perfect your pitching skills, but don't become too hung up on the outcome. Remember: if they don't pick you, pick yourself.
- Enter writing contests to distinguish yourself with decision-makers who can help your career.
- Maintain a strong online presence, which exudes professionalism.
- Don't complain.

CHAPTER 10 -
DETERMINING YOUR CLIENT'S NEEDS

"Talk to someone about themselves and they will listen for hours."

~Dale Carnegie

When you are in the business of selling your writing services, steer conversation away from yourself and toward your clients. Consider their needs. As a *$ix-Figure Writer*, you are often in the service business—*the service of others business*. Remember this truth, and you'll not only make your clients happy, you'll earn their money. This chapter discusses the importance of establishing clear boundaries, guidelines, and milestones. The best way to ensure a six-figure income is to position yourself for the next assignment.

A Word About Being Your Client's Therapist

Michael

When you signed up to be a *$ix- Figure Writer*, you also agreed to be the emotional sounding board for your clients. Perhaps this prospect bothers you. Maybe it intrigues you. If you can learn to embrace the privileged position of being an intimate confidante to your client, you can significantly grow your business.

How Does This Work?

Creative projects invariably entail a significant personal connection. In particular, if you take on ghostwriting assignments to pen someone else's memoirs or fictional books, you will find yourself absorbing some of their most private thoughts, memories, and observations. Because human beings are not robotic automatons guided by cold, rational determinations, a wide range of deep emotions may bubble to the surface throughout your exchanges. Your role, if you choose to accept it, is to respect the person's experience, listen, and find a way to shape the personal data into solid writing.

Delve Deep

Listen quietly, take notes, and ask questions in these meetings. Pursue each emotionally charged portion of a person's story with sensitivity, vigor, and focus. You may be in for some awkward, deeply intimate moments. A weeping client may tell you things they have never told another soul. Do not shy away from such intimacy. Seek the emotional truth. The more detailed, emotionally charged information you receive, the better. Your role as a *$ix-Figure Writer* is to draw out those private details which lead to the best writing. If you have to experience some uncomfortable moments along the way, so be it. Think about it this way: the juicier the details, the better the potential outcome.

Don't Get Personally Involved, But Don't Be a Jerk Either

As a *$ix-Figure Writer,* you must act professionally. Listen to disturbing stories from your clients with dispassion and without judgment. They contracted you to tell their story, not give them advice. Your therapist obligations only extend to listening to their tales without criticism. You are not there to fix their problems, nor should you try. Be courteous and respectful of their feelings. Do not take this responsibility lightly. You are being granted the awesome privilege to enter into hallowed, hidden dimensions few people have trespassed.

It would be a grave mistake for your professional career not to treat each aspect of these exchanges with anything but respect. Why? It all goes back to the *$ix-Figure Writer Axiom.* Every exchange between you and your client is a chance to build trust. Do not blow it by laughing inappropriately, or worse, stonewalling them with silence after they've just related their deepest secret. Instead, find a balance between being sincere and caring, but personally detached.

Loose Lips Sink Ships

Honor confidentiality. Even if the assignment is not a ghostwriting venture in which you signed a formal confidentiality agreement, treat it as such. Do not tell your client's secrets. You've been afforded a special privilege to be privy to personal information. Do not bite the hand that feeds you by running off to your friends to tell them the sordid details of your client's life. Not only would it constitute an unconscionable betrayal, it's bad business. Can you imagine anyone wanting to work with a person whom they do not trust?

***$ix-Figure Writer* Tip:** Earn a reputation for discretion by refraining from talking to others about your clients' personal information. If you happen to record sessions for creative purposes, turn the data over to the client once the project is completed.

Deliverables

The term *deliverable* comes from project management and describes a tangible or intangible object to be delivered to a client. Early in my career as a *$ix-Figure Writer,* I began using this term to denote items my clients could expect to receive through our working partnership. I advise you to do the same.

Definition of Deliverables

It is incumbent upon *you* to anticipate your clients' needs for each project. Never assume the client knows or even fully understands what is involved. Not only does it save time and misunderstanding if there is a potential dispute, it allows you to remain in the powerful position of determining what comes next and why. Though the client has contracted you for a writing project, always take the initiative to define what the outcome (final deliverable) should be, as well as what any milestones (intermediary deliverables) should include.

Short-Term Deliverables:

Otherwise known as one-offs, common examples include single blogs, articles, and essays. No matter what the assignment is, the idea the same: the work you are contracted to do is discrete. When you complete the assignment, you are finished.

In the next section, we will go into deliverables for long-term creative projects, such as books and screenplays.

Caution: Even if the assignment is just a small one-off blog, you still need a contract. The contract can be a single page, but it must include specific language listing the obligations of both parties. I've personally run into trouble by not defining explicitly what deliverables refer to in a contract. Learn from my mistake. Never begin work without an airtight contract containing specific language.

Long-term Deliverables Part One: The Need for Milestones

When doing long-term projects for clients, such as screenplay assignments, manuscript edits, ghostwriting commissions, etc. it is important to break the project up into intermediary milestones as opposed to one-off deliverables. This is important for two reasons:

- Communication. Both you and your client have an opportunity to check in throughout the creative process. The client may have crucial feedback better received sooner rather than later.
- Billing. Turning in deliverables, which are favorably received by the client, allows them to feel the project is on track. When they feel this way, it's far easier for you to receive your incremental payments as part of your total compensation.

Long-term Deliverables Part Two: The Intangible and the Tangible

The Intangible

The first deliverable for any long-term project is actually a bit of a misnomer. You won't actually be turning these deliverables into the client in written form. Think of the first (intangible) deliverables as the *brainstorm sessions.*

As the name suggests, brainstorm sessions are the crucial nascent stage of any long-term creative project. You and the client must meet face-to-face (preferably) or through another medium, such as Face-Time or Skype. I recommend the face-to-face approach at the client's home for two reasons:

- Ease. Speaking in person at a client's home allows you to take stock of all materials on hand you may need for the project. It also provides you with a personal sense of the client you otherwise might not receive if only communicating electronically.
- Personal connection. This relates to the first section in this chapter. The longer you spend with the client in person, the more opportunity you have to build a relationship. The better your relationship, the more details you'll receive to aid your creative project.

The major purpose of the brainstorm sessions is to paint a unified mental picture of the creative project: what it will entail and what the ultimate outcome should be. During these sessions, actively do the following:

- **Conduct Reconnaissance**. Think of yourself as a spy. It is your job to soak up and absorb every aspect of the project and the client to use as material. If it you are writing a book, pore over pictures, listen to stories, ask questions, etc.

- **Take Notes**. Bring a notebook or laptop and jot down anything you think may aid in the project. I also recommend recording these sessions to refer to them later.
- **Begin Shaping**. The next (tangible) step will be to begin the outline, but you needn't wait. While absorbing material from the client, concoct ideas about how to execute the project. You don't necessarily have to present your ideas yet. The important thing is to put yourself in a creative frame of mind.

The Tangible

Your brainstorm sessions are the precursor to the outline. The outline will be your new best friend throughout the long road ahead. To use another apt metaphor, the outline is a blueprint for the project you are building. Craft a sturdy, well-ordered blueprint, and you can expect a strong, beautiful result. If you take the time to draft a thorough plan of attack from the outset, you will save untold hours of frustration and heartache later on when creative problems seek to derail all your best-laid plans.

The outline is your first tangible deliverable to the client. It needs to demonstrate your understanding of the scope of the project and how to execute it. The more thorough you make this document, the better. For instance, if you are writing an outline (sometimes called a treatment) for a screenplay, include sample dialogue to give it flavor. Provide detailed descriptions of characters, tone, genre, and potential scenes.

This may seem like basic information for any working writer, but your clients will not be familiar with the outline's purpose. It will be up to you to explain it. As for those aspiring *$ix-Figure Writers* bold enough to begin a long-term project without an outline, good luck. It is a *huge* mistake not to organize your approach.

Once you've finished your outline, ask the client to sign off on it in writing. In the future, you and your client might disagree about some aspects of the project. If this dreaded day comes, you can point to their written approval as evidence that you are proceeding according to the plan you both agreed to.

A final note on this topic: make sure you put something in writing in the contract that states, "The outline is meant to be a structural aid in the writing process. It does not contain each element of the eventual project." This language will cover you in case there are necessary but unforeseen elements you need to modify later.

Long-term Deliverables Part Three: Intermediary Deliverables

Intermediate deliverables or milestone deliverables are vital to demonstrate you are making progress on the project to the client. These are opportunities to check in periodically. They allow both parties to gauge how you are proceeding toward the creative goals established in the outline.

Here's a practical example:

When ghostwriting a book, I bill monthly. I inform the client I will deliver two chapters (or approximately twenty pages) as milestones for their feedback on a consistent schedule. Receiving positive feedback from the client (preferably in writing) lets me know they are happy with the work as it progresses.

Long-term Deliverables Part Four: The Final Deliverable

To protect yourself, structure all your contracts so you receive final payment *before* providing the final deliverable: the polished product. It can mean requesting final payment when turning in a draft, which is 90% complete.

The reason I suggest getting this payment upfront is once you've turned in the final product, you will have no leverage other than the contract and the client's word they'll pay you. It may sound overly cautious to request payment this way, but my policy is "better safe than sorry." You don't want to have to chase down a client for payment after you've done all the work and have no leverage.

Long-term Deliverables Part Five: Problems

In a perfect world, you'll land Susie, the dream client. She will happily collaborate with you throughout the brainstorming sessions to craft a detailed outline that leads to well-received deliverables. You'll then deliver a final product she loves. Great! Job well done.

But let's say it goes differently with Susie. In this scenario, four months into a book project, there's a problem. Until this point, you have been in constant communication, getting written approval for each deliverable. Things are going swimmingly until you send Chapters 14 and 15 for her feedback (along with your monthly bill).

Suddenly you receive an email. Susie is unhappy with the book. What do you do?

Problem 1:

All the milestone/intermediary deliverables you've presented to Susie so far have been received favorably. Until now. Only the recent items are a problem.

Of the three deliverable problems, this is the easiest. The good news is you don't have to go back and rewrite the whole book, starting with the outline. Susie's problem in this instance is discrete. It relates only to these chapters and will not affect the whole book.

The easiest way to deal with the problem is to listen to Susie's complaints and suggestions. If they are easy and won't change the overall project substantially, agree to them without argument.

Problem 2:

The recent milestone/intermediary deliverables you presented to Susie were not received favorably. The changes Susie now wishes to make will affect not only these chapters, but may affect earlier chapters you've already written.

Contain the problem. If the changes Susie wants require a substantial rethinking of the material, don't panic. Though part of you may be tempted to yell at Susie for not bringing crucial items up when you created the outline together, don't. The best thing to do is listen to Susie's concerns.

If you've done your due diligence and received her written approval on the outline, point out she already agreed to the approach you are taking and nothing has changed. If Susie insists what she agreed to in the outline doesn't matter because what you turned in isn't working, still don't panic.

The best thing to do is to take a step back from the project for a day or two. Use this time to let your mind consider all the possible ways you can incorporate Susie's wishes without wrecking all the work you've put in. With a little inspired creativity and flexibility, you can still salvage the project and your relationship with Susie. You might even improve the material based on her insight.

Problem 3:

The milestone/intermediary deliverables you presented to Susie were not received favorably. The changes she wants to make will drastically affect the material. Not only do all the chapters need to be redone, the whole outline needs to be reworked from page one.

You've now entered the Danger Zone. How you proceed from here must be carefully thought out. You risk losing Susie's trust and approval if you go to war over these dramatic modifications. And yet, if you don't push back, you risk destroying the creative integrity of the project.

First, delicately remind Susie what she agreed to by signing off on the outline. Because the changes she wants to make negate the initial vision she agreed to, she's at fault for the current impasse. However, it'll do no good to point it out unless you do so tactfully. You are dealing with a person who is not being reasonable. It's therefore a mistake to try to reason with her.

At this point, you have only one option:

Swallow your creative integrity. Agree to finish the project based on Susie's new suggestions, even though they contradict your beliefs. Next, update the outline with Susie's new ideas and get her approval again in writing. Agree to the changes and complete the project as quickly and amicably as possible. Then move on. Do not agree to work with Susie again. You now know she is not a professional.

EXERCISE: How to Deal With an Unreasonable Client in the Middle of a Long-term Project

STEP ONE: Prepare for the worst. Before meeting or taking a phone call, think of all the possible things which could go wrong and how you might deal with them. Having this preparation in place will help prevent you from being blindsided.

STEP TWO: Relax. Take deep breaths before speaking. If you find yourself losing your cool and raising your voice, slow down or stop talking until you compose yourself. You will only make a bad situation worse if you further upset the client with unprofessional behavior (no matter how right you think you are.)

STEP THREE: Accept your limitations. You can't please everyone all the time. Accept it. Writing is subjective. Let go of feeling bad about not pleasing your client. There will be others.

Long-term Consulting for the Small Business Owner

We'll shift from long-term creative projects to long-term *practical* projects. One of the best ways to become a *$ix-Figure Writer* is to acquire clients who will pay on an ongoing basis. (This, of course, is difficult to achieve in the creative sphere unless you find yourself in the enviable position of writing an ongoing book or TV series.) Establishing consulting relationships with small business owners who can hire you indefinitely is ideal for selling your writing services.

If your writing talents lend themselves more toward the practical side of writing informative blogs, journalistic articles, or social media posts, you may be wondering how to create the optimal situation to receive consistent, ongoing work. I have one word for you: Retainer.

Retainers

The retainer approach is ideal both for small businesses and content writers. Hiring a marketing firm to promote a small business can cost a lot of money. On the other hand, today's businesses live and die by staying viable through social media. It educates their customers with stories, articles, blog posts, emails and newsletters. Content marketing. If you meet potential clients in the middle, it can be a win-win situation for both of you.

How to Sell This Idea to Clients

Tell your clients they can easily cut their marketing costs by dropping their overpriced marketing firm. Marketing firms carry huge overhead costs. You do not. There is no way that you are going to cost the client anywhere near the exorbitant fee these outfits charge. And yet, you can provide them with infinitely better marketing results.

Why? Overpriced marketing firms rely on antiquated advertising models.

The Overhead Marketing Scam

Mad Men portrays Madison Avenue conglomerates as sexy but their advertising model is as dead as their fashions. If you are familiar with this series, you may recall the clever trick Don's boss, Roger Sterling, pulled on their star client, Lucky Strike Cigarettes. For years, he billed his own advertising company's overhead to this one leviathan of a client. Lucky Strike was so bureaucratically overwrought and inefficiently run, no one caught on for years.

Today's small businesses don't have the working capital to support an overpriced marketing budget with limited results. They need quick return on their advertising dollars. They need value. If you position yourself correctly, you can be a one-person show for these businesses by being their in-house writer/marketer.

How to Sell the Retainer Idea to Clients - Part Two: Advantages

Your first thought should be: how can you *not* sell this retainer idea? The trick is anticipating your client's needs and then exceeding them.

1. Monetary Benefits

Your fee to be the in-house writer for items such as social media, ad copy, blogging, web copy, commercials, newsletters, etc. will be far less than any marketing firm.

This is not to suggest you lower your price. Instead, determine a figure a business owner would need to pay you monthly to take on all their written marketing. The rate should be competitive enough to convince the owner to choose you over a marketing firm, but high enough to be worth your time.

2. Precision Marketing

The antiquated marketing strategy of the last century was to throw ad money at a problem and see what stuck. We no longer live in the same world. Business owners can't afford to be wasteful and ineffective with their marketing budgets.

One of the benefits of online advertising is real-time analytics. Business owners can see for themselves who is visiting their site, how long they stay, and if they are converting. When structuring a marketing campaign with a *$ix-Figure Writer* on retainer, you and your client can strategically and precisely determine which marketing activities are having positive effects. Owners don't need to host complex marketing meetings with a marketing consultant to evaluate and discuss tactics. Instead, they can direct *you* to alter the approach. For instance, if blogs are getting the word out, write more. If customers are coming from the Facebook page, you can spend your time boosting Facebook posts.

3. Authentic Messaging

Having one writer on retainer as opposed to a bloated marketing firm ensures communications will come from one organized mind instead of many. Working on retainer, you have a great opportunity to determine the voice of the business you are promoting. In essence, you can become the fulltime mouthpiece through highly personalized, authentic messaging.

4. You Save the Business Owner Valuable Time

Here's a practical example: Let's say Kyle, the business owner to whom you pitch the retainer idea, says there is no way you can deliver his messaging as successfully as he can. He alone can communicate his business better than anyone else.

No argument. Of course, Kyle knows his business better than you do. After all, it is his business. But you can respond with this important question: how can he possibly find the time to run his business and market simultaneously?

If Kyle is realistic, he'll agree with you. It's not possible. The best use of Kyle's time is doing what he does best: running his business. Leave the marketing to you, the professional. It just makes good business sense.

5. If All Else Fails

If Kyle still balks, suggest he try it on an experimental basis. Ask Kyle to give your plan three months. If it doesn't work, he can drop you and go back to doing things his old way. But if Kyle accepts your offer, it will be up to you to prove your worth. Live up to your potential. Make Kyle so glad he hired you on retainer he'll never let you go. If you do so, congratulations. You have an ongoing, consistently paying client.

Chapter Summary

- Working with clients, especially on a long-term creative basis, can be a highly intimate experience. It is important to value the privilege of their personal and emotional disclosures with compassion and clear boundaries.
- Don't take confidentiality oaths lightly. Respect your client's privacy by not disclosing any personal information to others.
- The term deliverable is used to describe tangible or intangible content to be delivered to a client.
- Short-term deliverables, otherwise known as one-offs, include single blogs, articles, and essays.
- Milestone deliverables refer to intermediary deliverables to the client to indicate forward momentum on a project. They serve as a good opportunity for billing and to demonstrate the project is proceeding on track.
- Brainstorm sessions are the intangible deliverables, which facilitate the beginning of any creative project. They are ideal opportunities for the writer and client to collaborate on what the project will entail.
- The outline is the first tangible deliverable to the client. It lists the scope of the project and how it will be executed. The greater the detail, the better.

- The final deliverable is generally the polished written product. Bill the client before completion for the sake of payment leverage.
- The best way to obtain a consistently paying, long-term partnership with a business owner client is through a retainer. This is the ideal marketing strategy for a business owner since it can cut their marketing costs while still providing precise and authentic messaging.

Action Steps:

- Delve deep emotionally with clients on creative projects to receive the juiciest information for their project.
- Remain uncritical and sympathetic when engaging with a client who shares their personal information.
- Always respect your confidentiality oath about privileged information you receive during creative sessions.
- Be sure to include specific language in contracts as to both parties' responsibilities and obligations.
- Try to anticipate your client's needs and then exceed them.
- Use a thorough outline to plan your creative project and have the client sign off on it in writing.
- Determine a consistent schedule for presenting intermediary or milestone deliverables to the client for their approval.

- If a project goes sour when providing deliverables, remember to finish your work professionally and then disengage from future work.
- Sell business owner clients on the advantages of hiring you on retainer as an in-house writer/marketer to provide their brand messaging successfully and authentically.

CHAPTER 11 - SOCIAL MEDIA

"Think about what people are doing on Facebook today. They're keeping up with their friends and family, but they're also building an image and identity for themselves, which in a sense is their brand. They're connecting with the audience that they want to connect to. It's almost a disadvantage if you're not on it now."

~Mark Zuckerberg

If there's one key component in establishing yourself as a modern *$ix-Figure Writer*, it's your ability to use and leverage social media to build an audience. Ironically, social media platforms were built to give writers a massive edge in marketing themselves. However, many of us do not use them effectively. Even most bloggers do a poor job of taking advantage of the tools social media provides. In this chapter, I tackle social media and how it impacts you as a writer. Specifically, I explain how to leverage social media to benefit your writing ambitions.

Wasted Opportunity

Sham

So many writers and aspiring authors drop the ball when it comes to social media because they lack a comprehensive strategy. The tools to publish on social media channels are easy to use. We know it's not difficult to write a tweet or post to Instagram. The tricky part involves actually building a following and self-branding. This is where those who think like a marketer shine. Those who focus strictly on writing fail. It's simple. Those who put marketing first will successfully sell their work. Writers who stay hung up on writing at the expense of marketing will never get attention for their work.

Misplaced Priorities

Many writers struggle with social media because they focus on the wrong things. For example, most people mistakenly think only in terms of the number of followers they have, but engagement is far more important. Would you rather have 100 devoted individuals who read, *like*, and share what you post or 1,000 people who follow you but ignore yours posts?

Social media platforms form a massive ecosystem of communication and interaction on a gargantuan scale. Ripe opportunities for leverage lie dormant, just waiting to be exploited by forward-thinking writers. Powerhouse

Erika Mitchell aka E.L. James, the author of *Fifty Shades of Grey,* comes to mind.

Your ability to use social media effectively in a similar manner can be the deciding factor in writing success. Remember this: social media is the primary mechanism to cultivate and grow a devoted readership.

Primary Reasons Why Social Media is Crucial for Writers

Broadcast Your Work in Smaller Increments

Most writers think in long-form. Even when it comes to blogging, it's easier to write long than it is to be short and concise. However, social media is mainly designed for short-form posting. For example, Twitter limits you to 140 characters. Effective blog posts usually range from 400 to 500 words.

You can leverage this fact. By consistently sharing your writing in smaller chunks, you can put out more content by volume, thus increasing your opportunities to grow your audience. Conveniently, the emphasis on short-form material can also remove the pressure to produce lengthier engaging content.

Get Live Feedback Quickly

Fast response to your writing can be helpful. You can showcase what you are working on and get immediate reactions. Real-time feedback also aids in building anticipation and decision-making. For instance, ask your followers what kind of blog topics they want to read.

Engaging in this highly interactive way allows your readers to act almost like a personal critique group. The results will lead you to understand what resonates with your audience.

People-to-People Distribution

How often do you see your friends sharing content on Facebook or Twitter? Many times a number of them will even share the same article.

A huge component of social media is sharing content, whether news articles, entertainment, or my personal favorite, funny cat memes.

Social media allows for people-to-people distribution. When people share something, they're not just posting it to their page, they're broadcasting it to their followers for their personal consumption or interaction, such as with comments and *likes*.

The network model is built on the social way people behave in the real world. If your friends or family members share something with you, you will be more likely to give it your attention. This dynamic benefits you as a content creator, because every time you post something to your network, you have multiple opportunities for people to-people distribution, thus increasing your potential exposure.

Emphasis on Dialogue Over Monologue

Promoting is a monologue. It's like saying: "Hey. You there. Listen to my message." Traditionally, it has been a one-sided conversation in which the audience is expected to listen. Social media changed the paradigm by facilitating a dialogue *between* you and your audience.

Why is this valuable? Because you can interact with your readers, with your clients, with your customers. You can maintain an open line of communication; engage with them, have dialogue with them. Why do people follow public figures, celebrities, and athletes? They want to know what they're up to. They want to engage with people as fans.

Think about it this way. Have you ever interacted with someone whose work you admire, such as an artist, a fellow writer, or an entrepreneur?

How good did it feel to interact with that person? Really good, right? It probably increased your loyalty to their work and made you want to follow them more since you experience personal interaction. Social media is special because it gives you the ability to do the same thing. It offers a mechanism to provide a personal level of interaction.

Allows You to Be a Self-Branding Machine

Last, but definitely not least, you can use social media not just to build your brand, but also establish your brand identity. Social media allows you to convey exactly who you are and what you represent on multiple levels. It lets you showcase not just your work, your expertise, and niche, but it also lets you showcase your personality.

You can do this by posting content, by offering your opinions on things, sharing content you find interesting or valuable, and/or just being yourself. The last item is the key to personal branding. You have to be true to who you are. People aren't stupid. They can sense when someone isn't genuine. If you're trying to be something you're not, it won't work. This doesn't mean you shouldn't project some kind of false persona. It means your persona needs to be aligned with who you really are.

If You Build it, They Won't Come

Writers should thrive on social media. It plays to our strengths because we can create content with ease. In the end, our product is content, and writers are their own personal content factories. Yet, the problem is so much energy is expended in the wrong places.

Those who have a "writing first" mentality believe because they post well-written, engaging content people will find it. Those who have a "marketing first" mentality realize it doesn't matter how good their writing is if they don't have an audience for it. It's simple. Having a blog or a Facebook fan page doesn't mean anything if you don't have devoted readers. Just because you build it, they won't come.

There are bloggers with hundreds of brilliant, captivating posts, who get zero views. On the flip side, plenty of Internet marketers drive tons of traffic to their badly written, clichéd squeeze pages because they understand how to leverage social media.

To reiterate, writers should thrive on social media. This medium was built for our talents, and yet so many of use squander the opportunity. If you want to be one of the exceptions, here are two strategies to employ:

The Write Strategy

The Write Strategy involves using your writing in a targeted way across multiple social media *channels*. [Author's note: The term *channel* refers to different social media platforms, such as Facebook, Twitter, etc.]

The most important part of this strategy is knowing which channels are effective for writers and which are not. Which platforms to commit your attention and resources on and which you can ignore. For example, Instagram is more useful than Pinterest in building readership. Similarly, it's also more important to get a person's email address to grow your platform than it is to get a new Twitter follower.

The Commitment to Consistency Strategy

The Commitment to Consistency Strategy refers to the steady effort you must place on creating and posting content. Most people don't lack the motivation. What they lack is consistency. They want a large audience and thousands of followers. The difference between those who pull it off and those who peter out at a few hundred is due to the effort made.

If you want to grow a garden, do you plant the seeds and then water it once every few weeks? Not if you want to achieve maximum growth. A beautiful garden requires diligent care to thrive. Growing an audience on social media requires the same care. You must tend to your garden if you expect it to grow and yield any sort of harvest.

Channel Surfing

Social media platforms vary in name and primary functionality, but in essence, each is a channel for content distribution. It's important to implement a *multi-channel* approach to marketing and promoting your writing. Not all platforms are equal when it comes to their self-branding effectiveness for writers. Regardless of which channel you prefer; you need to leverage multiple platforms to establish yourself.

Most important, you must do the following things:

1. Determine which kind of content to post to which channel. Not all social media platforms are alike. Therefore, not all posts are applicable. For instance, what you post on Instagram shouldn't go on your LinkedIn profile.
2. Aim to share and create content, which can be adapted for distribution across multiple channels. For instance, if you write a blog post, you probably can't share the whole thing on your Facebook

profile. Instead, post a link to your blog. Then tweet the link.

Curated and Original Content

Although there are numerous channels, focus on only two categories of content: curated and original content. Let's go over each.

Curated Content

Curated content refers to articles, photos, videos etc. you share, which have been created by others. It's content you found engaging or helpful and want to share with your audience.

Original Content

Original content on the other hand, is anything you create.

Strike a Balance for Success

Effectively building your audience on social media requires leverage of both of these types in a healthy ratio. Obviously, it's much easier to share someone else's work. The amount of available content is endless. The problem with posting curated content too often, however, is that by doing so, you give away all the attention.

> **$ix-Figure Writer Tip:** When it comes to creating original content, it's most efficient to do it in batches.

> Block out time every week to brainstorm ideas and complete all your writing. (This could be for a blog post or for shorter social media posts. The rationale behind this approach is to have content ready to go.)

Reach vs. Followers

Building your audience is about getting eyeballs on your content. Too many people make the mistake of trying to get people to press *like* or follow. Instead, focus on audience reach. It's a horse before the cart situation. Followers come from reach. Focus on gaining the reach, and you'll get followers.

A little known fact about social media reach is you don't actually need many followers. Reach and follower numbers are not as closely correlated as people think. This was the guiding principle I used in building my own audience. For example, my digital media publication on vaping has 24,000 Facebook followers. But my weekly post reach has hit over 1.5 million at times.

Statistically, my follower count isn't very large (although for my industry it is the largest of other similar sites). Plenty of sites, like *Vice,* have millions of followers. To put it in context, I only have 24,000 people who follow my page. However, in a given week, over 1.5 million people actually see my posts in their news feed. And that's without any paid advertising or sponsored posts.

So What's the Secret?

I wish my technique were more impressive so I could seem much cleverer than I actually am. The secret, though, is what I outlined above: The Write Strategy combined with The Commitment to Consistency Strategy. I focus on reach, not followers. I don`t care how many people hit *like* because I know by default I`m going to gain followers if my posts are heavily distributed. As I mentioned, a number of digital media publications exist in my industry, but none of them are as consistent as my organization. What they post in a week, we post in a day.

To reiterate, successfully growing an audience on social media is about focusing on the right things, which yield results. Putting your emphasis on followers won`t bring you followers. Putting your focus on reach will organically gain exposure for you. The Law of Averages will do the rest.

EXERCISE: Obtain Curated Content

You need curated content sources for your chosen niche, but don't waste time every day scouring the web for interesting items to share. Here's how to maximize your time.

STEP ONE: Research. List five sources for content you happen to like and find useful.

STEP TWO: Subscribe to these sites and bookmark them.

STEP THREE: Check daily for curated content. You can also widen your net by saving items your friends and family share with you for later use. Take the early Christmas shopping approach here. Have items waiting in your closet (or desktop folders) for later use.

A final note: view everything you post to social media as an opportunity to provide value and engage with your audience. Remember the beautiful garden metaphor. By carefully cultivating a vibrant network, you will reap big rewards.

The Four Biggest Mistakes Writers Make with Social Media

By now, nearly everyone understands the importance of social media. Yet, just a few years ago, a lot of people weren't convinced. I recall in my days as a consultant, in the late 2000s to early 2010s, many of the businesses I worked with just didn't get it. It's hard to believe, but once upon a time, it was a struggle to get businesses to see the value in a Facebook fan page. Now, nearly every business of every type uses social media to their advantage.

The question is: are you using social media correctly for your writing business?

Mistake 1: Not Offering Value

Do your posts actually provide value to your audience? Far too many social media posts have no actual point to them. A random tweet does nothing for you. Neither does an irrelevant status update or a meaningless photo.

Attention is the currency of the web. Why should someone pay you some of their limited attention currency for a useless post? Why should they hit *like* or read what you posted if it adds nothing to their life?

When you share or post something on social media, it should offer some sort of value. Instead of posting: "Hey, I'm drinking a glass of water right now," try posting: "Three reasons why drinking water throughout your day is important." Then list them. Think about it. Do you care that I'm drinking water? Of course not. There's no value to that statement. But if I offer you some useful information about water, it could be worth some of your attention currency. Right?

Mistake 2: Begging Friends to Follow You

Don't panhandle for followers on social media.

Now, I'm not saying you shouldn't invite people you know to follow you. It's nice to have friends who show support. But this is not an effective long-term self-branding strategy. Ask: are they my target audience? Are they my potential customer base? Probably not.

Remember, followers matter. But the *right* followers matter more. It's a quality versus quantity issue. Having the people you know show their support is confidence building. But you'll never build a six-figure income from them. The key to social media success is online networking. By all means, leverage your friends and family, but don't waste your valuable energy trying to get them to follow you.

Mistake 3: Buying Followers

I'll come clean. I've done this before. I thought it was an effective way to grow my following. So I get it. You think it makes you look better to have someone following you. Ghost-followers are an accepted reality of social media. But buying followers for the sake of looking good is not wise and will hurt you in the long run.

Sure, you can buy Facebook *likes* with ease. But if you start building your followers this way, you'll greatly reduce the chance for actual fans to see what pops up in their feed.

Fake followers screw up your engagement, whether on Twitter, Instagram or Facebook. They lead to spam, attempted hacks on your profile, and other problems. Of course, it's tempting, but don't do it. There are no short cuts in social media and building an audience. Making it look like you have lots of followers is strictly cosmetic. Also, it looks funny if you have 10,000 fans on Instagram, but when you post something, you only get four *likes*.

Mistake 4: Lack of Consistency

This is the big one. Inconsistent writers create a profile, make a few posts for a day and then forget about it for the rest of the week. As I just said, there are no shortcuts when it comes to social media engagement. You have to be committed to consistently posting and sharing content. You have to make the time throughout the day, every day. I know it sounds tedious, but you have to do it.

People ask me how I grew my following for my blog. *Consistency.* My organization produced content around the clock, sharing, *liking*, commenting, engaging with our followers.

Far too many people start strong only to slack off after a week or two. It doesn't mean you have to surgically implant your smart phone into your hand and be on it 24/7, but you have to allocate the time and be active. Most importantly, you have to post daily. Nobody is going to follow you if your last post was from the month before.

Platform Overview: Which Ones to Use, Which Ones Not To

With so many social media platforms, it's confusing to know which ones to use. Since time is a finite resource, place your focus and energy on the platforms, which will yield the best results.

Must Use Platforms

Facebook: Of all the social networks, Facebook is the single most important for a writer. It gives you the most versatility in terms of post formats, has the largest number of uses worldwide, and it should serve as the focal point of all your online marketing.

Instagram: Although most writers overlook it as a photo-sharing site, there is a large and engaged community of creatives who share their work here. Its ample use of hashtags makes it easy to get your writing seen and discovered.

LinkedIn: The platform for professionals, it's necessary for networking and promotion. Networking is crucial to your career, and LinkedIn allows you to expand your reach beyond your local area.

Optional Platforms

Twitter: Many celebrities and thought-leaders use Twitter to engage with their fan base. It's definitely a useful tool, but it requires you to create a high volume of content to build a decent following. Approach Twitter only after you gain some momentum with the first three platforms.

Tumblr: By design, Tumblr's functionality seems perfect for writers. But the user base tends to be the very young, fourteen to eighteen demographic. Nevertheless, there is a decent community of artists and writers here. Tumblr can also be useful because it allows for niche and even micro-niche communities.

YouTube: How does a writer use a platform built around video? If your writing niche is non-fiction, YouTube is massively powerful for showcasing your expertise. You can make short instructional videos or a video series featuring yourself on your own channel.

Platforms Not Worth Pursuing

Other popular platforms, such as Snapchat, Periscope, and Pinterest are useful in their own ways. (For instance, Michael keeps his writing portfolio on Pinterest.) But they're not optimal for writers trying to build an audience. Therefore, I wouldn't put too much energy into them.

Chapter Summary

- Social media should serve as the foundation for promoting your readership. It's important you learn to utilize multiple distribution channels to market yourself and your work.
- Most writers drop the ball when it comes to social media and don't put in the required effort.

- You must build an audience for your writing. There is no exception. The way to build your audience is through social media.
- Social media provides people the opportunity to discover your work.
- Make a strong effort to interact and communicate with your readers in order to build rapport, trust, and engagement.
- Effective social media marketing requires consistency and daily effort.
- The key to building a large audience on social media is providing constant value and content that engages.
- Not all social media platforms are useful for writers. Allocate your time and energy to those which yield the best results.

Action Steps:

- If you haven't done so already, create profiles for all the main social media platforms.
- Make sure you create a compelling, attention-grabbing profile.
- Put all your social media focus on creating content of value to give people a reason to follow you.
- Allocate time every day to your social media activities. Remember the garden metaphor. You need to cultivate your network consistently.

- Embrace the power social media offers to broadcast and distribute your writing. This is the new paradigm. Use it to its full potential.
- Be on the lookout for content you can share with your followers. Your aim should be to enrich their lives.
- Become familiar and comfortable with social media vernacular and tools of the trade, like hashtagging.
- Always make time to engage and interact with people who follow you.

CHAPTER 12 -
BUILD YOUR PLATFORM

"Most people feel they are wasting time on social media or in developing their audience because they aren't focusing on the right people, on the right milestones, and don't understand how building an audience actually HELPS your writing progress.

People feel overwhelmed by all of this because they have no plan, no strategy. An author platform is about making hard choices on where to focus your energy, and is as much about what you DON'T do, as what you do. This is a process of refinement, focused intently on your goals as a writer."

~Dan Blank

Until the Internet, the ability to make your writing publically accessible required a lot of effort and approval by others. You could submit an article to a publication, but the decision to publish it was up to the people in charge. Blogging demolished the old paradigm. It placed the power to publish and broadcast in the hands of the people. It also opened the door for the democratization of self-publishing. In this chapter, we discuss the importance of building your platform, why it's so crucial for any writer, and how to accomplish it step-by-step. Authorpreneurship is also explained in detail as a significant and diverse revenue source to be leveraged and exploited via the platform model.

Why You Should Build Your Platform

Sham

We`ve discussed why it's crucial to build an audience on popular social media sites. But it is only half the equation when it comes to creating a viable online presence. In order to achieve a profitable career as a writer in the new Connection Economy, a *$ix-Figure Writer* must also build and establish a unique platform.

What does that mean exactly? Your own platform? Am I suggesting you have to hire a web developer and create your own social network?

No. It's not complicated.

Building your own platform simply means building an audience of your own, which isn`t dependent upon social media. Just as self-publishing allows you to release your own content free of the rules and constraints of a gatekeeper-style publisher, building your own platform lets you engage with your audience on your own terms, free of the policies of social media platforms.

But another key reason to build your own platform is important. It provides you a way to reach your truest, most loyal fans, the upper percentile of people who enjoy your work.

Your personal platform can be constructed using two primary components that work together:

- Your blog.
- Your email list.

Why Platforms Over Social Media

I'm not suggesting social media isn't important. But if I had to choose between having a large email list based on an engaged blog readership over a large social media following, I'd choose the first. Why? Because it's much easier to monetize a blog and email list than a social media following. Ideally, though, your aim is to make them both work together.

Your objective is to build a healthy, functioning eco-system. Any social media platform you participate in is in full control of the rules. Without warning, they can unilaterally change the way things work. They can even shut down or delete your account if they want to. I'm not suggesting it will happen, but it could. By signing up to use their platform, you agree to abide by their terms.

For instance, say you build a big Facebook following. Hypothetically, Mark Zuckerberg could wake up one day and decide, "Hmm... I don't like that page. I'm going to delete it." While accounts are rarely deleted, unless you do something wrong, what many social media platforms do is switch how they distribute content. Although social media is now a regular part of our lives, it's still a relatively new concept. Even behemoths, like Facebook or Twitter, have only monetized their platform for a few years. It's important to understand the way these platforms pay the bills is through advertising. Therefore, they are always in a state of flux, constantly tweaking and experimenting with new ways to advertise and reach consumers.

Consequently, the first goal of any social media company is to figure out how to provide the most effective advertising mechanism for their client businesses to spend their money on. If they have to sacrifice user experience to that end, they will do so. Facebook is infamous for sudden changes without warning in how it decides what to show in your news feed.

Remember, you may gain followers and build an audience on social media, but the platform is in charge. It's like purchasing a condo unit with a Homeowners Association. You can decorate it however you wish on the inside because it's your place. But you don`t control the Homeowners Association. You have to follow their rules. Building your own platform is different. You *are* the Homeowners Association. You set the rules.

Why You Need a Blog to Build Your Platform

Whether you`re trying to sell your writing services or your writing, you need a blog. No exceptions to the rule. Why? You need a place where you can post content and drive readers. Think of your blog as your business card. It establishes tremendous credibility. In fact, the only thing more powerful is to have a written book.

In Chapter 8, Michael touched on the need for portfolios. These can help you get writing assignments. Though a blog can be a part of your portfolio, it also provides something more. It shows people you have something of value to say, and it allows you to self-brand around your chosen expertise. It also creates the focal point for your own social media ecosystem.

TOP SIX REASONS WHY YOU NEED A BLOG:

1. It establishes your authority and expertise.
2. It allows you to build your personal brand and interact with fans of your work.
3. It drives traffic to your homepage.
4. It enhances your SEO (Search Engine Optimization).
5. It allows readers to opt in to your email list, thereby generating leads.
6. It supports and enhances your social media presence.

Blogs Allow You to Sell Stuff

Blogs are an effective way to sell items and make money. You can sell your services, your products, and once you build an audience, you can even make money from other people's products or services by promoting them.

Blogs allow you to create branded content. Providing original content does the advertising for you. If someone goes to your blog and reads a post, you don't have to promote yourself. By default, your value is being transmitted to the reader.

***$ix-Figure Writer* Tip:** There are a number of ways to make money as an affiliate. It needn't be your primary focus, but it can generate additional revenue. You can review products and sell them through your own unique link. You can earn a commission for sending referrals to other services. Amazon even offers a way to earn money for promoting goods purchased from them. Check out Amazon's affiliate program and www.clickbank.com for more information on affiliate marketing.

It All Goes Back to the $ix-Figure Writer Axiom

There's an important caveat to the discussion on earning money through your blog. The key to monetizing your audience with a blog is creating trust. You don't need to sell anything overtly. Instead, focus on establishing trust with your readers.

Trust is the social currency that drives today's Connection Economy. If you put money before trust, you'll be broke. If you put trust and value before money, you won't even need to try to monetize. It will happen naturally. We want to support people we like, people we trust.

The *$ix-Figure Writer* Blogging Formula

Your blog is the primary place to host and publish your original content. Once you publish something, distribute it through your social media channels. This drives traffic to your page, spotlighting your other content. (This is an SEO strategy. But inversely, with SEO, you optimize content for people who are searching for the particular topic.)

Greatly increase your reach by promoting posts. Facebook, Instagram, and Twitter all offer "sponsored" posts. This allows you to laser-target the audience you want to reach based on a wide variety of criteria, ranging from age to interests.

The foundation for your content factory, your blog is the focal point you use to host content and then drive traffic through it. Once you write a blog, distribute it throughout all your social media platforms. Be consistent with the formula and you will slowly, but surely, build your following and get traffic.

Note: Plenty of programs claim to teach you how to generate thousands of hits a day in web traffic. They're selling you nonsense. If there was some secret magical technique, I'd gladly share it with you. Take it from someone who has actually built a blog readership of thousands of readers per day, the key is patience and commitment to the long game. There are no short cuts.

How to Set Up Your Blog

Setting up a blog is easy. Setting up a blog, which actually looks good and has functionality, on the other hand, requires some technical skill.

We writers are able to evoke emotions with words and captivate with our prose. Yet we tend to have terrible design skills, which is why I strongly urge you to have your site professionally created by an actual web designer.

If you don`t know what you`re looking for, a designer will quote you higher prices for add-ons you don`t actually need. But have no fear. We`ll help you avoid these issues.

First, your blog can serve as your website. They`re pretty much one and the same. Also, asking a web developer to install a WordPress theme will yield a much lower quote than asking for a website to be built from scratch.

Your website will be built on what's called a "CMS" or content management system. The great thing is, the back end of a CMS is easy to learn, use, and navigate.

The most popular and widely used CMS for blogging is called WordPress. A "theme" is a pre-made website with modules. Once it's installed, you can customize it however you see fit. The great thing about themes is most of them come out the box ready to go.

What Your Site Actually Needs

You're a writer, not a startup company. All you need is a basic, simple website to promote your products and/or services and to showcase your blog. That's about it. Don't worry about the bells and whistles. Make your priority getting traffic to your site, which converts into an audience.

Next, it's important you clarify to your developer that you're looking for a WordPress theme installed, not a full-scale website setup. Where do you find themes? A number of online market places sell pre-made ones. My personal favorite is *Envato's Theme Forest* (not a typo) found at www.themeforest.com

Themes are relatively inexpensive, usually between $40 and $60. You can always use them, so it's definitely a great investment. Next, many places offer to install the theme for a small charge. Don't do it. It's not a bad service, but you're still going to need some custom work. (This is why I strongly advise you to find an actual web developer.)

Where do you find a web developer? Some online marketplaces list freelancers. Services like www.Upwork.com and www.Freelancer.com are safe bets.

Simply place your bid and your budget. A quality developer should charge between $300 and $500 for the work. Note: you can save some money by outsourcing the work to people in other countries, but I don't advise it.

Find somebody local. You will get much higher quality work when you can actually sit down with the person face-to-face. Last, don't fall for scams by big agencies which quote ridiculously inflated prices.

***$ix-Figure Writer* Tip:** There are DIY website builders like *Squarespace* or *Wix*. They aren't necessarily bad, but they limit your reach, especially with SEO. They're a better fit for local businesses, which simply need an online presence for marketing purposes. You need an actual blogging engine optimized for searches. Save yourself the headache and don't try doing it yourself.

Hosting and Domain Registration

A website needs a place to host it. You purchase server space for a small amount every month. It's where your website will actually be stored. A very common newbie mistake involves signing up for hosting along with registering your domain. This isn't necessary. You can purchase your domain @ www.yourname.com without purchasing hosting. In fact, you can purchase hosting from a different place than where you registered your domain.

Most hosting companies offer "free domain registration" when signing up for a hosting account. This sounds great, and you save about $10, but the domain host technically owns your web domain. This means you can't just cancel and switch over to a different host. You'll need to transfer it, which is an annoying process.

Instead, I urge you to register your web domains at one place and host them in another. In the end, it's a smart precaution not to have the two interlinked. Last, my preferred domain registry is www.NameCheap.com. I have used them for years. They have great prices and feature very easy to use services.

EXERCISE: Generate Your Site Map and Web Copy

To save time and money, have a site map ready for your developer. You should also have your web copy prepared. This exercise will help you create both.

So the first question is, how many pages do you need and why?

A writer needs the following pages:

Home Page: This should be your blog. The first thing people should see is your content.

About Page: Share your story and your background. Provide a little insight as to who you are and why you're awesome.

Services: List a brief summary of what you can provide.

Books or Products: If you're a self-published author or you're selling any kind of information program, have a page that showcases your work and links to buy it.

Contact Me: Provide a quick and easy way for people to reach you.

Portfolio: Include sample content here.

Final Tips: Make sure you have buttons linking to all your social media accounts and share buttons for people to share your articles.

You MUST have an email opt-in box somewhere on your page.

Email Marketing

There is one final important step to build your own platform: capturing emails. I said followers aren't as important as reach. Your email list is actually more important than your reach. Why? Your email list is the lifeblood for any writer. Without an email list, you don't have a platform to begin with. The more email addresses you acquire, the larger your audience will grow. When combined with a healthy social media following, you are well on your way to establishing your brand.

The reason email addresses are so important is they guarantee a way to contact and stay in touch with subscribers. Most people check their emails consistently and rarely change their email address. Next, emails ensure reach. When you post something on social media, not everyone is going to see it. It either doesn't show up in their activity feed or they just miss it due to the sheer volume of posts they have to contend with. Email may not be as interactive or as engaging as social media, but it gets the job done.

$ix-Figure Writer **Tip:** You may assume social media has overtaken email in terms of marketing effectiveness, but the numbers say otherwise. Social media provides more reach, but email still has the higher conversion in terms of generating actual dollars.

But Will They Actually Open the Email?

Maintaining a vibrant email list will ensure your message goes out to your audience. But simply sending an email doesn't guarantee the recipient will actually it. This is why trust is important and you need to craft attention-grabbing headlines. Another powerful strategy is to make sure your email service provides custom, personalized names included in the email title. An email with the recipient's name has a 29% higher open-rate than one without according to Experian Marketing Services' 2013 Email Market Study.

How Do You Actually Get People's Email Addresses?

What you don't want to do is just ask people for their email addresses. Think about it. Why should people give you their email addresses? People hate spam. You have to offer something extra as incentive for readers to part with their personal information, something compelling enough to make them opt in and give you permission to keep contacting them.

The most effective way to do this is to create your own exclusive content and then offer it in exchange for an email address. This can be done in the form of a quality newsletter they will only receive in exchange for an address. The strategy is simple: keep some of the good stuff for the people who are willing to entrust you with their addresses.

Should I Get an Email Service?

Definitely. Mail Chimp is the best in my opinion (www.MailChimp.com.)

Infusionsoft (www.InfusionSoft.com) is also very good, but it has some expensive bells and whistles you may not need.

These types of services can provide you with pre-made sign-up boxes your web developer can quickly add to your site, along with some professionally designed email layouts. They also have the ability to customize your lists and organize. Set up an auto-responder to send a thank you email to people who sign up on your site automatically.

> **$ix-Figure Writer Tip:** An exclusive newsletter can be a highly effective email marketing technique. They range from monthly, bi weekly, or quarterly, though monthly tends to be the most effective. It's a great way to stay in touch with your readers and/or clients while also helping to enhance your brand.

A Final Word on Design

You may need a logo or some design work completed for your website. Freelancing sites, such as Upwork and Freelancer, are great places to start. Another is www.99Designs.com. It allows you to post a project. Designers can then bid on it by sending you ideas.

DON'T cut corners. Words may be our medium of choice, but design is important. They say don`t judge a book by its cover, but today, the packaging is key.

Rise of the Authorpreneur

Now that you have built a successful platform, it's time to take advantage of it. One of the best ways is to self-publish, entrepreneur-style as an *authorpreneur*. Wait. What is that?

An authorpreneur is a writer who approaches authoring books from the mindset of a business enterprise. Many individuals, such as Jay Boer, author of the *New York Times* best-seller, *Youtility*, are not writers by trade, but rather consultants and speakers who use authorship to establish themselves as Thought Leaders in their field, using a strategy called expert positioning.

By now, you know there is no better business card than having your own ebook. Many experts write and (self)-publish in order to gain credibility, which can often segue into rich opportunities for diverse revenue streams.

Diverse Revenue Streams

If you're a consultant or life coach seeking to set yourself apart from your competition, there's no better way to position yourself as an expert than to write a book. The ease of self-publishing makes it good business sense to write a book and self-publish.

Another variation to the authorpreneur strategy is to build a business around your writing itself. Many self-published authors, such as the talented and prolific Joanna Penn, author of the *Arkane Action Adventure Thrillers*, do this by writing an ongoing series. Penn, who writes under the pseudonym, J.F. Penn for her fiction, is unique because she authors non-fiction books for writers as well, such as *How to Make a Living With Your Writing*.

To go back to Jay Baer for a moment, not only do his books earn him an income on their own, but he has successfully parlayed his well-deserved perception as an expert consultant into keynote speaking gigs all over the world for thousands of dollars. The founder of *Convince and Convert*, he also consults companies on gaining and keeping customers "through the smart interaction of technology, social media, and customer service." The key takeaway from his model is the writing Baer does is only *one of his revenue streams*. He has successfully found ways to stretch his authorpreneur monetization efforts to encompass multiple income streams.

The "Preneur" in Authorpreneur

One of my favorite sayings about entrepreneurship is, "An entrepreneur is someone who's willing to jump out of a plane with no parachute and build one on the way down." It's a good way to summarize the gutsy, yet innovative mindset of people willing to risk it all on the idea that they can be successful in their own business.

What is a business? A business offers one of two things: it sells products or it sells services. The interesting thing about the authorpreneur business model is it has the potential to tap into both revenue streams. Authopreneurs can sell their writing as products and/or they can sell their services, such as consulting and speaking. These are legitimized by their authorship.

A Low-Overhead Model of Perpetual Passive Income

A daunting concern for many entrepreneurs is the required capital, especially for creating inventory. For instance, if your business is selling cell phones, you first have to pay for the materials and the cost to produce them. That's a big investment to incur with no guaranteed return. But what if you had a product with no cost to you except your own time and energy? This is the beauty of the authorpreneur model.

Best of all, once you create your product, you can sell it again and again at no cost. Write it once, profit from it forever. Just ask bestselling author, Andrew Weir. *The Martian*, his initially self-published novel, is continually raking in cash and has been adapted into a blockbuster movie. Can you say passive income? Authorpreneurship sounds like a dream business model, doesn`t it?

Another aspect to this evergreen model of perpetual passive income is Authopreneurs can build upon their monthly revenue stream through a consistent output of ebooks, which create a backlog. The more they build their audience, such as by continually adding satisfied readers to their email lists, the more opportunities they have to sell their content through backlogs.

Consider this idea from the Law of Averages perspective. Say your one ebook sells 100 copies a month. Now imagine you also write a new ebook every month for a year. You`ll then have twelve books selling 100 copies a month. Your evergreen content will compound on itself, creating more and more revenue. And remember: it'll only cost you the time and energy to produce it. For more information about becoming an authorpreneur, listen to the *Authorpreneur Podcast* hosted by Jim Kukral through the Rainmaker Platform.

Chapter Summary

- In order to ensure long-term success and career stability, you must build an audience through your own web platform.
- Every writer must have a blog where they regularly and consistently publish their own original content.
- Your blog should serve as the focal point for all your marketing and branding.
- Once you build an audience, you can monetize your blog.
- Your goal should be to establish and cultivate trust with your readers.
- Growing an email list is a necessity for your career as a *$ix-Figure Writer*.
- Invest in a quality website for your blog.
- Similar to social media, consistently provide value to your audience via your blog.
- An Authorpreneur is a writer who approaches book writing as a business in the manner of an entrepreneur.
- Any writer who wishes to self-publish must think and operate as an authorpreneur. Your writing is the product you sell. However, there is also an added opportunity to create additional revenue streams via self-publishing by marketing your consulting services.
- Technology has made it easy to produce and publish large volumes of self-published, backlogged titles to be leveraged as evergreen sources of perpetual income.

Action Steps:

- Obtain a high-quality WordPress website developed by a professional web designer.
- Keep your website simple and easy to navigate.
- Set up an email opt-in that allows you to grow your email list.
- Brainstorm and create some exclusive content to incentivize readers to sign up for your email list.
- Have your designer index your site for SEO so your articles show up on Google.
- Get acquainted with popular self-publishing platforms, like Amazon`s KDP and CreateSpace or MOBI or Kobo.
- Brainstorm the niche or genre for which you could write a book.
- Look through Amazon`s Kindle store to determine what kind of self-published books are selling the best.

CHAPTER 13 -
HIGHER EDUCATION: TO GET A DEGREE OR NOT

"Formal education will make you a living; self-education will make you a fortune."

~Jim Rohn

"One of the greatest obstacles to escaping poverty is the staggering cost of higher education."

~Chris Van Hollen

Sham and Michael hail from different educational backgrounds. Sham went to college for business but didn't complete his degree. Michael holds a B.A. from the University of Missouri and an MFA from Chapman University.

Higher education isn't cheap. It's helpful if you wish to become a *$ix-Figure Writer,* but it isn't a prerequisite. In this chapter, we'll each discuss the pros and cons of higher education when it comes to your income goals. Sham will present the pros and cons of *not* earning a degree while Michael will explore the pros and cons of earning one.

Michael will close this chapter by offering a third, innovative option for aspiring *$ix-Figure Writers.*

MICHAEL'S PERSPECTIVE

The Traditional University Experience

I loved college. It was the best time of my life. I had the quintessential male university experience: living on campus, pledging a frat, pulling all-nighters, studying abroad, partying, attending thought-provoking lectures, going to homecoming, football games, dances, etc. My two years of grad school were great, too. I lived in another charming college town. I got to walk to campus and participate in intensive writing workshops with advisors like David Ward, Oscar-winning screenwriter of *The Sting.*

A lot of what I just mentioned centers upon the social aspect. If I am honest with myself, the reason I enjoyed school so much was because of the people I met, the friends I made, the girls I dated. I even married my wife after meeting her at a Chapman mixer. I also learned a great deal at college. I received high marks and achieved the Dean's List every semester. The personalized screenwriting instruction I received was hugely beneficial. But now, I am out of school and away from all the parties and fun, and I must ask myself tough questions: was my education worth all the money? Was it worth going into debt?

I'll explore the ramifications of my decision to seek higher education. It's my hope that relating my experiences will help you decide on your own path.

PROS:

College Taught Me to Think Critically and Produce Abundantly

The level of college discourse is lightyears away from high school. College is where you learn to think for yourself. You will need this skill in order to be a successful *$ix-Figure Writer*. You will also need the practice of meeting deadlines and preparing thoughtful essays.

I was fortunate to study in England my junior year. Instead of frequent quizzes and assignments like the American educational model, we were required to write one major paper per subject per semester. Of course, the papers I turned in had to be outstanding. My essays were all heavily researched and included references as well as a substantial bibliography. I mention this because so much of the writing I do now as a *$ix-Figure Writer* is based on the skills I fine-tuned in college.

My professors expected highly structured papers containing correctly attributed quotes to substantiate whatever point I was making. Without the extensive practice I received in critically thinking about ideas across diverse academic subjects, I would be hindered in my ability to write long-form, intelligent articles and books such as the one you are reading.

The requirements of college molded discipline. College forced me to produce abundant work on deadline.

Here's an instance. During my freshman year, I caught the flu right before finals. I had a big Political Science paper due. If I didn't turn it in, I would flunk the course. Yet, I was so ill I was practically delirious. I couldn't fail, so I drank Nyquil one night after ingesting a strong dose of antibiotics. Then I purged the sickness by sweating it out in the campus sauna until I felt well enough to concentrate. The next day and night were hell. I sat in the computer lab for hours, typing away until I completed the full assignment. I received an A on the paper and an A in the class.

The point of that story is college prepared me to focus on outcomes when it comes to obligations. My professor would not have accepted sickness as an excuse. Similarly, my clients don't accept excuses either when it comes to delivering on things I have promised.

My MFA Degree Taught Me How to Write Professionally

Before entering Film School, I had never read a professional script or written a technically correct screenplay. I did these things numerous times during my writing-intensive MFA program. Just as instructors encourage total immersion when learning a new language, MFA programs expect you to turn in vast amounts of material on deadline.

The other crucial component of my MFA program was the feedback. Whatever deficiencies or abilities I had as a screenwriter, technical or otherwise, were discussed with peers in roundtable groups. With the exception of my instructors' feedback, these critique groups were the most helpful aspect. I heard my own words read aloud by my peers in real-time. (The way this works is that the author assigns parts to be read, like a casting director, including someone designated to be the narrator.) After the material was read, my instructor led the group in constructively evaluating what worked, what didn't, and how to improve the writing.

This kind of hands-on, immersive experience, in which I was constantly reading not just my own work, but also the scripts of others, taught me the technical mechanics of good writing. I discovered how to best craft good dialogue, sympathetic characters, and compelling storytelling.

Though my MFA writing program was expensive and featured top professionals in the entertainment industry, such as Ron Friedman, screenwriter of the original *Transformers* movie, as well as Ross Brown, Executive Producer of *Step By Step,*. the experience felt cooperative, rather than competitive. It fostered important relationships.

My MFA Writing Program Helped Me Form Key Relationships

Beyond the educational, practical aspects of an MFA degree, another huge component was the friends I made. Writing can be a lonely, solitary endeavor unless you are collaborating. The benefit of attending a structured writing program was it forced me to interact with others on a consistent basis. By providing and receiving helpful feedback, I forged important relationships that have served me well.

Due to the nature of the film industry, the relationships I formed were crucial to gaining jobs and/or writing assignments. For instance, I'm particularly grateful to a friend, Karin, from my MFA program, who recommended me for a professional reader position at Creative Artists Agency upon graduation. She opened a door in my career by vouching for me.

My wife and I often joke we paid thousands of dollars for the friends we made in our MFA program. However, there is some truth to the statement. Just like fraternity pledges who grow close or army cadets who develop strong ties from surviving boot camp, my fellow students and I bonded over adversity. My advice to anyone entering an MFA program is not to overlook the important social component. Befriend everyone. You never know who can help you.

An MFA Degree Sounds Prestigious

People are impressed when I tell them I have an MFA degree. As mentioned, perception matters to the earning capacity of a *$ix-Figure Writer*. Whether we like it or not, we live in a society defined by status and images. Most people we meet do not bother to take the time to know us. They react to the image we project: how we look, what we wear, how we talk, what we drive, where we went to school, the degree we earned.

Being able to tell potential clients I earned a Master of Fine Arts Degree has been a boon for me professionally. I often trade on this background. It instantly signals credibility. To be sure, an argument could be made that anyone can buy a higher education degree. To some extent, this is true, but a level of competence and ability is required from graduates at accredited institutions. The important takeaway is: perception matters. We may wish it were otherwise, but this is the reality. This book is about how to play the game, not question it.

CONS:

Higher Education is Insanely Expensive

Here are two frightening statistics to give you pause:

> *"The average 2015 college graduate will owe approximately $35,000 in student loans."*
>
> ~*Edvisors.*
>
> *"The ticket price for a 2-year MFA program (including room and board) per student is around $100,000."*
>
> ~*The Atlantic*

It's important to consider higher education with open eyes. I just elaborated on the benefits of earning an undergraduate and a graduate degree, but it's equally important to be candid about the downside. In recent years, college costs have ballooned. According to the College Board, the average cost of tuition and fees for a private, nonprofit, four-year university in 2015 was $31,231—up sharply from $1,832 in 1971-1972 (in current U.S dollars). At public, four-year schools, tuition and fees cost about $9,139 in 2015. In the 1971 school year, they added up to less than $500 in current dollars.

Since the price of college has increased exponentially, it's worth considering not going to avoid the enormous debt. Put it this way: if you owe $100,000 in student loans coming out of college, your debt will cripple your earning potential for years. Unless you become a *$ix-Figure Writer* immediately, you'll be plagued with steep monthly payments. They will make it difficult to save money, much less buy a house or any other large purchase. As opposed to other forms of debt, such as credit card, you cannot discharge your student loans under current bankruptcy laws. You must ask yourself, "Is it worth it?"

A College Degree Does Not Guarantee a Job

Higher education used to open doors for graduates. Not so much anymore. The unfortunate reality is college is no guarantee against not having a job. On the flip side, many employers won't even consider someone who doesn't have a degree.

The other unfortunate reality is a degree in the Arts, such as English, is even less valuable than a business degree. I can't think of one potential employer who looked at my degree in Philosophy as a plus. On the other hand, when I went into business for myself, many people who commissioned me as a writing consultant (not a W-2 worker) appreciated my Philosophy degree. It often impressed their creative sensibilities.

This leads me to my disruptive conclusion. While it's true that traditional employers are no more prone to hire you for having an undergraduate or graduate degree and probably even less likely to hire you for possessing a writing degree, you don't need them.

Being a *$ix-Figure Writer* is not about playing it safe. So-called "safe" jobs no longer exist. We live in the Connection Economy where pensions are no longer guaranteed and job security is a joke. If you decide to go to college or earn your graduate degree, do it on your own terms. Do it for the education you will receive, the contacts you will make, and how it will look to the clients you intend to work with some day. Do not do it to impress a future boss. It won't work anyway.

This innovative thinking leads me to an unorthodox solution for the *$ix-Figure Writer,* a third path for so-called higher education. Look for it at the end of this chapter.

SHAM'S PERSPECTIVE

Why I Don't Regret Not Going to School

I've always had an odd love-hate relationship with academics. I love to learn, but I never liked school. I love education, discussing ideas, theories and thought. Yet sitting through long lectures was akin to waterboarding for me. I can sit and read for hours on end, but studying a textbook puts me to sleep.

Ironically, as much as I disliked it, I always did well in school. For me, it was never a problem with learning. It was a problem with structure. I love the environment of school. The energy in any college library was always intoxicating: people sitting around in the warm, brightly lit building, surrounded by books, drinking coffee or tea, diligently reading, writing, and dissecting knowledge. I just never enjoyed the actual structure of school. My problem was if it was a topic I actually found interesting, I'd learn everything possible about it. But if it was a subject I didn't find stimulating or engaging, I wouldn't bother. Why waste the brain space if something isn't interesting or useful?

In high school, I did independent study halfway through my sophomore year. I was truly lucky to have the opportunity to do so because it removed me from the normal school structure. My instructor was wonderful because she gave me a level of control and flexibility as to what I studied. This program also allowed me to skip class, which sounds odd to say in retrospect. But from about fifteen-and-a-half, I was out of the traditional school system.

Instead of going to school, I worked. As soon as I was sixteen and eligible, I worked fulltime and took classes at the local community college. My most formative adolescent years were spent in the "grownup" world. While most of my peers got drunk for the first time, I worked with adults and went to college.

I tried numerous times to commit myself fully to school, to be a fulltime student and get a business degree. I'd enroll with a full course load and start the semester strong. Then I'd just stop showing up to class. Sounds reckless, if not ignorant, but I was young and didn't see the point. My biggest problem was I didn't have enough interest or enthusiasm to sit through boring general education classes I knew I wouldn't need. My other problem was I knew a lot of older successful business owners, and all of them had the same opinion. A degree was nice to have, but they didn't do much with it.

I never intended to work for anyone. I always knew I wanted to be an entrepreneur. I realized having a degree didn't offer much of an advantage when starting my own business. It's not as if upon graduation, business students get $50,000 to start their dream business. If anything, it's the opposite. You leave college in debt.

I'm not suggesting you shouldn't pursue higher education. What I am saying is for certain professions, you don't need a degree. In some of those professions, having a degree can hinder your chances for success by saddling you with debt before you begin your career.

This isn't a debate over book smarts versus street smarts. Any intelligent entrepreneur knows the value of applicable knowledge and the power of reading. But they also know the value of experience over theory.

I'm older and have gained experience as a serial entrepreneur, and I can say with certainty you don't need a degree to start a business. Furthermore, having a degree is not a prerequisite for a writer. Most of my friends are highly educated and have advanced degrees. I truly admire them for their commitment and hard work. But I love to tell them, I'd eat them alive if they tried competing in my industry as an entrepreneur.

Succeeding as an entrepreneur requires grit, determination, self-reliance, the ability to think outside the box, and most importantly, a willingness to ignore the rules and do your own thing. I applaud the amount of effort and perseverance earning a degree requires. It conditions you to function within a system. If you follow a set curriculum with a natural linear progression, you'll have a roadmap to follow and gather people along the way to guide you.

Making it as an entrepreneur, on the other hand, is a sink or swim situation. You have to be able to operate free of preset parameters on your own merit. School can teach many things, but it can't teach experience. Even degrees, like marketing, are useless, because what actually works and what's taught in textbooks are completely different.

When it comes to earning a degree in the field of writing, the situation is the same. You may gain a more thorough and proper understanding of syntax and grammatical structure in college, but you won't be taught how to build a prosperous career from your writing.

I've never found my lack of a degree a hindrance to my career as a consultant. Nobody ever said, "I want to work with you, but you don't have a college degree." A degree can be useful, but do you know what's more useful? A reputation for success and a proven track record.

I'd never tell someone who wants to be an entrepreneur not to go to school. What I say is, don't expect anything from it except being able to tell others you have a degree.

And never think school curriculum will make up for experience.

Say you are a business owner and you want to hire someone to create an effective marketing strategy for your company. You have two candidates. Candidate A is highly educated and has just completed her MBA degree. However, aside from an internship, she has no work experience. Candidate B never finished college, but she has a decade of experience launching successful companies, including some of her own. In addition, Candidate B has a proven track record of marketing and branding success. Who would you hire?

PROS:

You Can Save a Lot of Money and Disappointment

The universal complaint all my friends who completed advanced degrees have is their student loans. The nice thing about getting people to invest in your business is you often don`t have to pay them back. They invest, and if things work out, they benefit from their ownership percentage. If the business fails, you aren't obligated to pay back the debt. It's the investor's loss. All investors know how it works.

A business loan is different, of course. You have to pay back a business loan, but with so many willing investors today, you can raise capital for your business by promising equity and profit share. On the other hand, there is no way to avoid paying back *student loans*. Even if you file for bankruptcy, your student loans won't be discharged. So no matter what, you'll have to repay the debt.

Another rude awakening many students encounter is disappointment in the realization their degree doesn't provide much except eligibility to apply for higher paying jobs. Having a degree might make you feel special until you consider the sheer number of people with your same educational level who are applying for the same jobs. This assumes the company *wants to hire someone for a fulltime position.* After all, they could as easily pay a consultant like me to do the work for less. Based on this reality, it's no surprise freelancing is on the rise. It further levels the playing field between college grads and those with actual work experience.

Then there are the dream-crushing hoops employers make you go through even if you played by the rules and got a degree. For instance, I have a friend who is a very talented engineer. He's like a calculator when it comes to mathematics. He finished his master's degree a year ago and finally located a job with a good firm. I took him out to lunch to celebrate, and my jaw dropped when he told me it would probably take him another ten years to advance to his desired position.

The corporate world truly kills dreams. I feel blessed to be in my position. It's alarming how many friends went through the rigors of college only to have to work at entry to mid-level positions at companies where they're miserable. I picture what that must feel like and cringe for them. They have to dress up every day, kowtow to the higher-ups, and be told what to do and when. Most of all,

I think about the nonstop stress and grueling workload just to work for someone else.

Meanwhile, I sit in my sweat pants and sneakers all day, free to pick and choose the projects I want without any headaches.

You Learn Self-Reliance

By taking the entrepreneur or *authorpreneur* route, you're on your own. The benefit is the results are under your control. They will come from the amount of energy you put into marketing yourself. If you don't hunt, you won't eat, but if you hone your hunting skills, you might not just eat. You could feast.

All this comes down to you, of course. Nobody else can determine your success on this path except you. As a result, you will cultivate a level of self-reliance, invaluable in today's shaky economy. We all know job security is a fairytale. It hasn't existed for years. No job is secure anymore. Those who went to school and followed the traditional approach of earning degree to get a good job will still be vulnerable.

But you, as an entrepreneur, as a *$ix-Figure Writer*, can take matters into your own hands. You can establish your own consistent revenue stream based on your passion for writing.

You Pursue Your Dream Much Sooner Than Later

Life is short, and the amount of time you have is not guaranteed. So why wait to chase after your dream?

Obviously, if your dream is to be surgeon, you need to hit those books. Then again, you probably wouldn't be reading this if that were the case.

You won't be a *$ix-Figure Writer* overnight without substantial effort. It took Michael and me a lot of time, energy, sweat, and coffee to get here. As much as I love to mention sitting in my sweat pants all day and making money writing, you should know what's required. We worked hard to achieve our dream and still continue to do so. But the daily thrill of waking up and doing something we love doesn't seem like work. It feels truly magical.

In choosing our own path, we accepted responsibility for our destiny. Whether you succeed or fail is in your hands. You're aligned with your higher purpose. You're aligned with your passion. Chasing a dream can be tormenting and turbulent, but it beats mundane, frustrating dullness. And it's a whole lot better than the stress of working a soulless, nine-to-five job just to pay the bills.

A *$ix-Figure Writer* isn't just someone who earns a secure living from writing. The money is great for security. We all know food costs money. Life costs money. The real reward isn't the substantial income, it's the fulfillment of doing what you love and realizing your dreams.

CONS:

You Sometimes Feel Inadequate

Most of my friends not only earned undergraduate degrees, they also completed graduate and PhD level programs. I won't deny I sometimes feel a little insecure at parties and social gathering. A level of prestige comes with earning a degree. You miss out by not going to school. Take my esteemed and awesome co-author. You probably take Michael a lot more seriously than you do me. It's far more impressive to say you're an MFA-possessing writer than an entrepreneur/blogger.

Has my lack of a degree ever stopped me from being taken seriously? Never. Even my most educated friends come to me for business advice. Intuitively, they know experience and credibility always trump degrees. Nonetheless, if you decide to forego higher education, you must make peace with it and not regret it.

An Innovative Solution to Becoming a $ix-Figure Writer

Internships: Or What You Should Consider Instead of College

Forget about internships being slave labor. If you want to get into the realities of socio-economic exploitation, a far more compelling case may be made that college (in the US anyway) is socially approved indentured servitude.

A viable alternative to college is a solid internship. An internship can be a great way to find work, gain experience, and build relationships. As opposed to college, internships cost nothing except your time.

Why are internships so helpful? No one expects much from an intern. Interning is advantageous because of its perceived low expectations. You are there to learn. Presumably, you aren't being paid, so no one fusses about firing you if you don't immediately catch on to the responsibilities of your position.

Think about it. It's a win-win for you and your employer. Interning means you are offering to work without pay for someone just because you like the good work they're doing. This statement alone can't help but ingratiate you to the person you wish to intern for (if you say it an authentic way.)

Another reason internships are helpful relates to college. What do most people receive from attending four years at a university? Theory. As you know, theory is not the same as doing. Interning is analogous to apprenticing. It allows you to train under a mentor, to discover firsthand how to succeed. If you happen to intern for a company and a position opens, the company may be willing to hire you (especially if they like your work.) This can be an invaluable first step to beginning your career, though you shouldn't settle for working for someone else in the long term.

Possible internship opportunities to consider include social media marketing firms, production companies or even journalistic outfits. At the very least, if no one eventually hires you, your internship mentor will likely write you a good recommendation letter and vouch for you to potential employers. My own internship at a production company led to my first entertainment job at Creative

Artists Agency based on a recommendation from a friend and a letter from my mentor, Cindy Cowan.

$ix-Figure Writer Tip: If an actual internship position doesn't exist at the place you wish to intern, contact the person you want to work for, and try to have a position made for you. It couldn't hurt.

The best way to use this life-hack solution is to play it both ways. Intern while going to school to get the best of worlds: the legitimacy and education of higher learning, combined with technical, on-the-job experience. Last, if you decide not to pursue higher education altogether, intern somewhere to improve your six-figure earning prospects.

CHAPTER 14 -
TIME MANAGEMENT

"If you don't write when you don't have time for it, you won't write when you do have time for it."

~Katerina Stoykova Klemer

"He who every morning plans the transactions of that day and follows that plan carries a thread that will guide him through the labyrinth of the most busy life."

~Victor Hugo

As a *$ix-Figure Writer*, the most precious asset you have besides your creative mind, is your time. The reality is the more you network, the more writing assignments you'll get. But you also need to factor in huge blocks of time to accomplish all your writing.

It's a delicate balance. You must carefully budget your writing assignments and networking activities in order to be truly successful. You can't put too much time into just one activity or you will fail to grow your business. This final chapter delves into these concerns as well as practical time considerations, such as how to manage multiple projects through batching to stay productive. Last, the practical mechanics of scalability are discussed to grow your now thriving writing business.

Procrastination: The Enemy of All Your Beautiful Ambitions

Michael

No book on profitable writing would be complete without some mention of this dreadful habit. The word habit cuts to the core of this issue like no other. Serial procrastinators acquired bad habits they never bothered to fix. In the previous chapter, we discussed the benefits of higher education to establish solid habits for producing content on deadline. If you didn't receive the benefit of such an educational structure, you need to establish your own internal discipline.

Next, if you are one of those unfortunate people who rely on others to motivate you to write, drop the habit this instant. The difference between successful and unsuccessful writers is largely due to their willpower and output. It would be silly to believe that any *$ix-Figure Writer* can expect to achieve success without having an inner disciplinarian, constantly pushing them to write. No one can do this for you. *You* have to make yourself write consistently and competently until the work is finished.

Writing vs. Networking: A Juggling Act

In Chapter 5, we discussed the need for a pipeline in order to bring in new work consistently. Then, in Chapter 7, we went over the importance of networking in order to attract more clients. We will now marry these important concepts with another vital consideration: quality time management.

All *$ix-Figure Writers* must split their time between two primary activities: networking and writing. This is not an easy juggling act. Strong writing involves uninterrupted time, deep thought, and intense focus. On the other hand, in order to reach the point where people pay you to focus so hard, you must interrupt your writing schedule to attend one-to-one meetings and social events. So, how do you make it all work?

It's Called Batching

I first came across this concept when reading Tim Ferriss's influential self-help book, *The 4-Hour Work Week*. Frustrated by time-sucking email, Ferriss implemented a revolutionary system. He assigned limited times for writing and responding to email. Through batching, he relegated all the hours he would devote to this activity (as well as others), preventing them from forever eating up his days. I suggest you employ the same concept for your writing and networking to be most efficient. It's what I do with my own scheduling, and I can't recommend it enough.

How This Works

Remember I said you don't need to write every day? I lied. Actually, I didn't, but the truth is more complicated. You must think of your business hours as a nine-to-five obligation. Put in *at least* eight hours every weekday either writing or networking.

If you aren't doing this, you shouldn't call yourself a working *$ix-Figure Writer*. Would you call someone a banker who works from two p.m. to three p.m. on Saturdays with the occasional Friday session thrown in from nine a.m. to one p.m.? Of course not. You might call them a part-time worker, if you were being generous, but a professional keeps professional hours.

Social Days & Writing Days

Let's say you have a networking breakfast every Tuesday morning from eight to nine a.m. with the Chamber of Commerce. On Thursdays, you meet with your BNI group from one to three p.m. Label Monday and Thursday your "social days." Since it's impossible to have uninterrupted writing sessions these days, you might as well devote them to batching *all* your social networking for the week.

The other three weekdays: Monday, Wednesday and Friday, are for scheduling your writing batches.

$ix-Figure Writer **Tip:** Batch schedule your networking on "social days" and your writing on "writing days" to create the ideal workflow.

Use Every Day to the Max

Within either assigned batched days, try to cram as many possible activities associated with your respective tasks.

For instance, if it's a "social day," schedule back-to-back social meetings with clients during the other available times. Don't just do a business breakfast on Tuesday. Cram in a networking luncheon, too. Tuesday night, go to a mixer. In between functions, make follow-up phone calls to your leads or check in with people who can grow your business. This is also the time to send email to clients and potential clients you may have put off to focus on your writing.

On batched "writing days," don't schedule any social engagements. Avoid checking your email and turn off your phone. (At least until you have completed the assignments you've set for yourself.) Hunker down and use every precious batched writing minute to be as productive as possible.

One More Thought About Batching Your Writing

Some writers think they need to be in "the zone" to produce good writing and will wait for inspiration to strike. Stephen King has an apt response to this: "Amateurs sit and wait for inspiration, the rest of us just get up and go to work."

This is the mentality you need as a *$ix-Figure Writer*. You don't need to write every day, but you do need to put in at least eight hours of writing each day, five days a week, just as you would at a regular job, if you expect to be paid like a person who holds a regular job.

To return to our metaphor about bankers, the same logic applies. It's absurd to imagine a banker waiting for inspiration to begin banking. *$ix-Figure Writers* hold themselves to the same professional standards. They schedule times for writing batches and complete their assignments during those hours.

It'll All Work Out

If you're worried about not feeling inspired or in the zone, don't be. Worrying won't solve anything. While your conscious mind is occupied with all kinds of menial tasks during the week: scheduling meetings, paying bills, running errands, etc., your unconscious mind is still hard at work solving your creative problems.

Creative solutions and inspiration will come to you during your downtimes: when you're in the shower, walking your dog, or driving to the grocery store. If you stay on task and batch your time, you will accomplish everything you need to do. *And* you will put out great work.

Manage Multiple Projects Like a Pro

When I tell people I am writing multiple books at the same time across genres, while consistently taking on various short-form creative content assignments for the web, they are often surprised. Some people have the idea the human mind can only focus on one major creative project at the same. Don't believe it.

When I worked as a commercial insurance broker, I would switch tasks sometimes ten-to-fifteen times an hour. For instance, I would be drafting a renewal proposal while researching umbrella pricing. The phone would ring, and I would have to explain the claim status to a property manager. Before I even hung up, I'd notice an email from my supervisor saying I had to FedEx a policy before the cut-off time.

Did I go to pieces with all these competing tasks? Did I tell my clients it was simply too much to expect me to handle their questions and manage their billing? Of course not. Somehow, I got it all done *because I had to.*

You need to act accordingly as a *$ix-Figure Writer.* The advantage is you love being a writer. I despised being an insurance broker and wanted to quit every second. Having the *luxury* of managing various writing projects is a good problem. Do you know what an honor it is to be a paid working writer? How many people would think they had died and gone to heaven to face such concerns instead of the tedious drudgery of their current jobs?

Practical Advice

The easiest way to handle multiple projects is to approach them the same way you coordinate your writing schedule: batching. Essentially, you are batching *within* batching.

Here's an example. Let's say today is Monday, your writing day. You've committed yourself to eight hours of writing. Simply break up your schedule into discrete tasks. From eight a.m. to noon, work on Project A. From one to five p.m., do project B. Avoid overlapping the two projects. It's great to multitask errands. It's a terrible idea to multitask writing projects. Complete your work for one project and then move onto the second.

Deadlines: Under-Promise, Over-Deliver

Always do this with your clients. Here's a practical example of how to use this technique. Let's say you are attending your Tuesday morning Chamber of Commerce breakfast where you interact with both potential and current clients. You happen to run into Jack, a current client. He commissioned you to write copy for all his monthly newsletters for the next year, starting with January. It's currently mid-December.

Because you were wise to take the above scheduling advice to heart, you have already decided to write the year's content in one long, batched assignment. Instead of having the obligation to complete Jack's newsletters one-at-a-time each month for the next year, you are going to take the pragmatic approach. In your mind, you plan to knock them *all* out in one eight-hour batch writing session.

Jack says, "When can I expect to receive January's newsletter?"

In your mind, you know you'll probably be done with January's newsletter (as well as all the other newsletters for the year) by next Tuesday because you plan to do a batch session on Wednesday. Then, during Friday's batch session, you will edit all the work you put in on Wednesday so it's grammatically perfect and compelling to read. Most likely, *all* the work will be done by Friday evening at the latest.

Do you tell that to Jack? No. What's the correct response?

"I will have January's newsletter to you next Tuesday by 9 a.m."

Let's Breakdown Your Answer

It's important to note you didn't say, "I *should* have January's newsletter to you next Tuesday by nine a.m."

Saying *should* as opposed to *will* violates the *$ix-Figure Writer Axiom*. Remember, you always want to build trust, not erode it. *Should* is wishy-washy. It conveys hesitancy and lack of certainty. Amateur freelancers tell their clients they *should* have their work to them. *$ix-Figure Writing* champs inform their clients when they *will* have their work to them. It's concrete. It's definitive. It gives the client one less thing to worry about.

Next, why is the correct answer Tuesday and not Friday when you will most likely be done with the assignment? You don't know what the future holds. You haven't started the newsletters yet. You don't know what they will entail. Perhaps they will be harder to complete than you foresee. Your plan is to finish them on Wednesday, but what if you don't? What if you have a family emergency that saps the time you intended to complete the assignment and you have to do it all on Sunday instead?

Of course, you don't want to tell these internal concerns to Jack. For one thing, Jack has his own problems. He's a struggling business owner, focused on his chiropractic clinic. He commissioned you to remove a task from his schedule. Besides, perception is everything. If Jack has to wonder if you are reliable, you've violated the *Axiom*. You tell Jack he can expect the work on Tuesday so you can do two important things:

- Budget in extra time for unforeseen problems.
- Make yourself look good when you actually deliver the work early.

Over-delivering to a client is one of the best things you can to do to create goodwill. What a nice surprise it will be for Jack when you actually deliver *all* the content (not just January's newsletter) on Tuesday after you proof it and make sure it's perfect. Not only will you have satisfied your client's expectations, you will have exceeded them.

Last, the final reason this is the correct response is its time specificity. You didn't just say Tuesday or even Tuesday morning. You gave an exact time. It's helpful for the client because it gives him one less thing to think about. Jack doesn't have to wonder when he can expect his deliverable. You have given him a concrete expectation.

Scalability

At some point in your illustrious rise to the top of the *$ix-Figure Writing* game, you will come to the inevitable conclusion there is only so much writing you can physically accomplish on your own. There are only so many hours in the day you can apportion to taking meetings and socializing. You're just one person. Or are you?

Multiply Yourself

The fact is your potential earnings are hampered by logistical constraints. Even if you are a writing rock star, like Monica Leonelle, who can produce 4,000 words per hour, there are a finite number of hours in a day. You also need to sleep and do all the other things that make life worth living.

Never fear. You can multiply your writing efforts (and your earnings) by hiring other writers to work for you. In Chapter 5, I suggested you create your own writing company. All the quality work you have done, all the goodwill you have earned in your rise to the top as a *$ix-Figure Writer*, is associated with your company. When the glorious day finally arrives when you are not only earning six figures, but actually cannot keep up with the demand for your services, you will be in the enviable position to outsource yourself.

Delegate But Don't Forget Your Brand is You

Let's say your niche is writing social media copy. You climbed the ladder of success by impressing clients who loved your work. You crafted engaging posts and brilliant blogs to convey your clients' messages in skillful, yet authentic ways. All your efforts have paid off so well you have to turn down jobs because the demand is so high. This is a good problem to have.

First of all, don't turn down jobs. There's no point in leaving money on the table when your goal all along has been to get to the place where your own writing can give you the life you want to lead. Instead, hire a likeminded writer (or writers) such as yourself. Carefully vet each individual you hire for ability and dependability. The last thing you want after working so hard to build your brand is to tarnish it by bringing on someone who doesn't share your values.

EXERCISE: Questions to Ask Applicants When Interviewing Writers to Work for You

QUESTION 1: What are your writing strengths?

This question will determine which categories you can delegate. You probably will choose to do the big creative projects, like ghostwriting books, if it's your niche, but you may wish to sub out social media content if you can find applicants with the necessary skills.

QUESTION 2: Do you have experience working on deadline?

Don't just ask this question. Test the applicant with an assignment and see if they can follow through with a quality piece of content on time.

QUESTION 3: What subjects do you like writing about?

Use this question to determine a candidate's knowledge base. If you learn an applicant has experience blogging for the fashion world, you now have a better idea of potential items to assign the person.

Personally Oversee Everything

The best way to ensure the work you're subbing is top quality is to review the content personally. If you need to make edits, do so. It's your company, after all.

At this point, you will come to the surprising recognition you are not just a writer, you are an editor and manager.

It might rub you the wrong way, especially if you are a purist about your writing, but it's essential if you want to scale your business to new heights. Since you can't possibly take on all the potential writing work your efforts have wrought, you need to accept you are now a business owner with subordinates you must manage.

A whole chapter or even a book could be written about the topic of delegating when it comes to writing, and we are working on it. For now, the important takeaway is to scale your writing company. In order to do so, leverage your success by bringing on other writers you trust to complete the work. Note: your contacts will still recognize you as the face of the company. As such, you'll be responsible for your underlings' output. Therefore, don't just vet all potential writers, but proof all the writing they produce. After all, your image is on the line.

One last thing: if you have gotten to this point as a wildly successful *$ix-Figure Writer*, congratulations. You are amazing. There may even come a time when you need middle managers to supervise all the writers you've hired to replace yourself. If and when that day comes, you have truly arrived. We will address this situation in future books. For now, pat yourself on the back. You've just completed the *$ix-Figure Writer* guide. Now follow the plan.

Chapter Summary

- Procrastination is the result of poor habits. It needs to be managed immediately if you have any real intention of becoming a *$ix-Figure Writer.*

- There is no room for amateurs who need inspiration to get motivated when it comes to earning a living as a professional writer. Professionals don't wait for inspiration to write. They simply do their assignments.

- An effective way to structure your time is *batching,* the setting aside of certain hours for specific tasks.

- Successfully balancing networking and writing can be a tough juggling act. One of the best ways to organize your workflow is to batch "social days" strictly for networking and "writing days" for long, uninterrupted writing sessions.

- When handling multiple writing projects, it is vital to batch *within* batching. Designate times within a given "writing day" to work on one specific assignment at a time before moving on to the next.

- The key to exceeding client expectations is to under-promise and over-deliver.

- The best way to scale your writing business is to hire writers to take on additional assignment so money is not left on the table. Vet these writers and review all their work as they represent your brand.

Action Steps:

- Hold yourself to an internal discipline when it comes to your output. Never procrastinate.
- Juggle networking and writing obligations by grouping your days into specific, respective batches in which you complete tasks.
- Try to use every available minute within your assigned batch days for maximum time management.
- Handle multiple writing projects simultaneously by batching *within* batching for utmost productivity.
- Under-promise but over-deliver when it comes to providing content.
- Always be specific about times/dates when informing a client when they can expect their deliverables.
- Be sure to work at least eight hours a day, five days a week as a writing professional.
- Avoid worrying about inspiration for your creative output. Learn to rely on your subconscious when it comes to generating solutions.
- Grow your business by scaling. Hire other writers you can use to delegate the work.
- Vet each writer who works for you to ensure the quality of your brand.

ACKNOWLEDGEMENTS:

As stated in Chapter 5, "Every successful book requires a skillful editor, who works with the writer to ensure the final product is in top shape before it's sent to market." This book is no exception.

We wish to thank our fabulous editor, Lorna Collins, for all her efforts in shaping this material. Her superb insight, trained eye, sagacity, and years of practical experience were invaluable. For more information on hiring Lorna professionally to edit and format your book, you may contact her at www.lornalarry.com or email her at 31months@cox.net.

We would also like to thank Sommer Stewart, our excellent designer, for the beautiful book cover. If you wish to reach Sommer to design your own cover and/or assist with your branding needs, you may reach her at sommerlynn@slyconcepts.com.

www.ingramcontent.com/pod-product-compliance
Lightning Source LLC
Chambersburg PA
CBHW070226190526
45169CB00001B/96